A Lyrics on Lockdown Anthology
2004 - 2008

A collaboration between Blackout Arts Collective, Rikers Island Academy,
The Community Learning Initiative at New York University's Gallatin School of Individualized Study,
The Institute for Research in African-American Studies at Columbia University,
& Eugene Lang College The New School for Liberal Arts

Edited by Lauren Bille & Danielle Lauren
Guest Editor: Ella Turenne

André Maurice Press | Blackout Arts Collective
New York

Published by André Maurice Press, an imprint of Owo Foro Adobe
ProJones.com

Lyrics on Lockdown is a program of the Blackout Arts Collective

Book Layout: Timothy W. Prolific Veit Jones Edwaujonte (projones.com)
Cover Artwork: Crystal Clarity (CrystalClarity83.com)

ISBN: 978-0-9779623-2-7

Library of Congress Control Number: 2008903869

Copyright © 2008 by Rikers Island Academy, Danielle Laura, & Lauren Bille. All rights reserved. Printed in the United States of America. No part of this book or e-book may be used or reproduced, stored in a retrieval system or transmitted in any form or by any means electronic, mechanical, photocopying, recording or otherwise, without prior written permission except in the case of brief quotations embodied in critical articles or reviews. For information, please contact the publisher.

10 9 8 7 6 5 4 3 2

Table of Contents

Publisher's Note	i
Editor's Note	iii
Introduction	vii
Poverty is a Mother	xiv
Love	**4**
Death	**61**
Lockdown	**78**
Revolutionary Pedagogy	125
Resources	147
Acknowledgments	149

Publisher's Note

It's folks that look like me
folks that think like me
it's folks just like me
locked down in prison

It's folks that made mistakes
I know I can relate
because it's folks just like me in prison.

— Michael Molina, Blackout Arts Collective
Lyrics on Lockdown Tour 2002

In 2002 I was introduced to **Blackout Arts Collective (BAC)** shortly after transferring to Hunter College as a young poet seeking to do more with my art than entertain college crowds. Within my first year of membership, I was educated by my peers about the Prison Industrial Complex, and Blackout's unique approach using art as a medium to educate and mobilize. The 2003 *Lyrics on Lockdown* (LOL) tour changed my life. Being exposed to individuals such as Bryonn Bain, Michael *Warrior* Bonds, Laurent *Tippy* Alfred, Ella Turenne, and Piper Anderson provided me with tangible examples of how to utilize artistry as a basis for education and to pursue social justice.

As a LOL participant, I performed in various poetry/hip-hop venues in New York & Washington DC, and conducted workshops with middle and high-school students, as well as with brothers and sisters caught in the system. My experiences on tour, which included stops at Rikers Island in New York, and Oakhill Juvenile Detention Center in Laurel, MD, shaped my vision both as an artist and as an activist. Every conversation with the brothers in Oakhill and every dap from the homies at Rikers are etched indelible on my soul.

The material written during the LOL tour led me to self-publish my first chapbook, *Explosion of a Dream Deferred*, which shared a title with a piece I had dedicated to the attendees of the performance at Rikers. The company I created to publish this book was André Maurice Press (AMP).

As both the publisher and designer of this book, I would like to explain some of the choices made with the text. Each piece has its own voice, and my goal has been to represent that voice through design, despite that I have not had the pleasure of meeting the majority of the contributing artists. My efforts to capture that voice have been through what I like to call creative formatting. I believe poetry to be a visceral and living art, and the words of the poets in this text prove that. Many of the statements made through these poems should be graffiti testimony on the halls of police stations, state and federal legislatures, and court buildings.

I am proud to announce this amazing body of work as AMP's inaugural release, which I find fitting as it was my relationship with BAC that allowed the dream of AMP to be realized. As the designer of this book, its publisher, and as the Co-Chair of the Board of Directors of Blackout Arts Collective, it is my pleasure to present to you an anthology of words, images, and lesson plans that personify the movement to abolish the Prison Industrial Complex. These are not adjectives or nouns, they are verbs. This is a book of action, love, pain, and truth.

To the brothers on lockdown: you are never forgotten.

We are here when you come home.

Uhuru Sasa! (Freedom Now!)

Timothy William *Prolific* Veit Jones
President/Founder
André Maurice Press

Co-Chairman of the Board of Directors
Blackout Arts Collective

Editor's Note

Activism cannot exist without transgression, and art is activism's greatest accomplice. Positive political activism requires the acknowledgement and redistribution of privilege and power. The editorial decisions made in the creation of this book were in constant tension with the roles of democracy, representation, egalitarianism, censorship, and authority. Yet conflict contains the quality of fire, it burns until transformation occurs, and in this case practices the vigilance necessary to maintain effective and fair political relations. Such is the work of collaboration.

Lyrics on Lockdown (LOL) utilizes artistic collaboration as a tool for praxis, theory and action occurring all at once. It is the shovel that digs deep when a two-hour lesson plan is chiseled down to twenty minutes. It is the space where the language of the classroom and the streets mix, and acquire each other's strengths. We want impact. We want connection. And yet the work is simultaneously complicated and powerful due to the acts of transgression occurring: privileged college students commuting to a high school within a jail to serve and learn, and Island Academy students, incarcerated on Rikers Island, daring to trust and engage when they have been repeatedly mistreated by systems within our society. Though built with positive intentions, these spaces are unstable; the societal class-gender-race relations affect all interactions within workshop time.

The instability keeps all involved on our toes. As one anonymous Island Academy student expressed during a free-write:

> *What set's me off? You asking me what sets me off sets me off! Do you really care about what sets me off? You've just met me, you don't even know my last name, asking me what makes me mad. Ask me my favorite color or something. In all honesty, if I ask you what I wrote here tomorrow would you remember? That sets me off, frontin' and fakin' sets me off.*

Fortunately, due to the classroom guidelines created as a social contract at the beginning of every workshop, we are able to have space for imperfection, interpersonal heat, and even conflict-- making the art more powerful, and the workshops more dynamic. This spark is what makes the hour commute to Rikers, plus the two hours of lobby sitting, plus various other forms of waiting and/or disappointment, worth the effort. A spark only needs the right question in a discussion, or the perfect prompt for a free write, and there is ignition!

Upon combing through four years' worth of lesson plans and free-writes, one student's words stood out, offering a fitting structure for the anthology. Cypress wrote, "*There are three kinds of pain: Love, Death, and Lockdown.*" Thus, all subsequent artwork fell into one of these three categories. Within "Love," we see themes of home, truth, and hip-hop. Within "Death," we find themes of struggle, pain, and style. Within "Lockdown," we trace themes of justice, judgment, and revenge.

When students are incarcerated at Rikers, the credit of any work that leaves the Island is restricted to the artist's first name and last initial. In the spirit of solidarity, we decided to note only the first name of every artist within the sections "Love," "Death," and "Lockdown." Furthermore, since the vast majority of the pieces were untitled, we decided to continue in the spirit of collaboration and format the writing so that each piece both stands on its own, and flows as part of a collective work.

Any reader who takes the time to page through the entire book will notice that one can still distinguish non-incarcerated members based on their gender. This subtlety, like the decision to use only first names, is a mark of another important dynamic in the LOL experience. While all of the members of LOL on Rikers Island are male, the majority of college participants are female. This gender dynamic is revealed in the following pages. We opted not to censor, since the program is meant to empower through transformation.

As mentioned above, the workshops that produced this art were constantly constrained by time. With this in mind, we edited each piece with the intention of maintaining its integrity as an expression of vernacular, literacy, and artistry, only changing words and grammar that strayed from each particular pattern of articulation. Beyond being an anthology, we wanted this book to serve as a sort of handbook for others wishing to achieve social justice through the arts, thus we provided a resource section introduced by ice-breaker-specialist Ella, complete with lesson plans, booklist, websites, and organizations to check out.

We would like to draw attention to one last subtlety that, if not mentioned, might be overlooked. On the inside cover of this book is printed a chart of the juvenile criminal (in)justice system provided by the Prison Moratorium Project. If you look closely, you will see the complexity of the system and the many ways that non-violent, innocent, juvenile, and/or first-time offenders can get lost for reasons as simple as not being able to afford bail or being in the wrong place at the wrong time without a proper advocate. This book is a medium for self-advocacy, and solidarity.

Finally, in the process of submissions, one LOL member requested that her thirteen-year-old nephew's writing be included in the anthology. It was the wording of her request that encouraged us to place Johnathan's piece as the outro to the book. She wrote, "Although he didn't participate in LOL, it is another voice familiar with all that we've been talking about." We predict that he is part of May and Bryonn's "next generation...writing its own future and beating back the penitentiary with the pen and the pad."

Many thanks are due: to Island Academy students for trusting us enough to stretch their bodies and minds, and stretching ours in return; to Bryonn for starting the wave and keeping the spirit of collaboration alive; to May for writing passionately and living her words; to Timothy *Prolific* Jones for his dedication to social justice through the arts as a publisher and poet; to Columbia students for creating an anthology that inspired; to New School students for keeping the dialogue going as LOL completes another successful semester; to NYU for funding this project, and NYU students for delving into the work; and to Ella for her zip-zap-zoom and smiling while stressed. You all know the fire well.

To our readers, thank you for collaborating with us. Allow yourselves to envision the hand that holds the pen, and the face behind the words. This is the work of re-humanizing.

Danielle Laura & Lauren Bille
Editors

Introduction

Maytha Alhassen & Bryonn Bain

"P.S. I'm not a Criminal."

These words ended a letter written by a teenager attending high school inside the world's largest prison colony. This young man's "P.S." was one of the countless revealing observations shared during the *Lyrics on Lockdown* course offered at Rikers Island since 2003 by Columbia University, NYU and the New School University.

If crime is a political definition, then who is the real criminal here? This young man with an entire lifetime still ahead of him? Or the society that mid-wifed the crack epidemic and drug policies that punish those whose lives are devastated by it? How about a government providing poor housing, overcrowded schools with underpaid teachers, and inadequate health care for military veterans and millions of other citizens? Those responsible for locating more liquor stores in working communities than grocery stores? Or a corporations invested in the warehousing of the unemployed and mentally ill while turning enormous profits from their slave labor?

The more heinous crime, of course, is the criminalization and incarceration of this teenager, and the snuffing out of passion, intellect and the uncultivated human potential of men, women and children like Jeff surviving in prisons nationwide. The following year, this eloquent student, too young to vote or enlist in the army, left his khaki jumpsuit and lace-less orange "Pataki" shoes at Rikers, but returned home with him the scarlet letter "C" tatted on his record.

Since 2001, Blackout Arts Collective has organized live performances and workshops to correctional facilities in 25 states during the annual *Lyrics on Lockdown (LOL) Tour*. LOL began as a summer tour, spawned a national campaign, and is now an innovative university course utilizing the arts to develop practical life skills, critical literacy and analysis of the prison industrial complex.

> *The term "prison industrial complex" was introduced by activists and scholars to contest prevailing beliefs that increased levels of crime were the root cause of mounting prison populations...Prison construction and the attendant drive to fill these new structures with human bodies have been driven by ideologies of racism and the pursuit of profit.*
>
> -Angela Davis

In a Rikers Island Academy workshop last Friday, several high school students in this Spring's LOL class agreed: if they had been able to afford their own lawyer, rather than using a court-appointed attorney who encouraged them to plead guilty as the only option, they would have known their rights and avoided being locked behind bars. As prison researcher Sasha Abramsky observes, "Big-time criminals go free..." after they trade valuable information, snitch out subordinates, and hire million-dollar lawyers who defend their client's freedom by any and all means necessary.

As the Enron execs and Karl Roves of the world go free or get the proverbial slap on the wrist, the poor and working people of color who comprise the bulk of the prison population serve the lengthiest sentences for possession of federally deemed "illegal substances." In the controversial case of Kimba Smith, for example, this young woman was sentenced to 24 years after her boyfriend coerced her into carrying his drug money across state lines. Indeed, women are filling up correctional facilities in America faster than any other demographic.

Yet over forty years after the tragic assassinations of Martin Luther King, Jr. and Malcolm X, race and class continue to be primary determinants of incarceration in America. With the spread of increasingly draconian drug laws, racially discriminatory enforcement mandatory minimums and three-strikes-your-out sentencing, the U.S. prison population has doubled -- and then redoubled twice more -- since the 1970s. Exploding from 200,000 to over 2 million incarcerated people, add those under parole and probation and over 7 million are currently under the jurisdiction of the criminal (in)justice system.

Despite a dramatic drop in crime across the nation, a 2007 study reported that despite differences of race, gender, ideology, age, region, political affiliation, income, and geography, Americans still believe crime is on the rise. If only 11% of the prison population is locked up for violent crimes then what is the source of this fear? The "fear industry" in the United States is steady "hiring lobbyists and subsidizing academics who, in turn, persuade journalists to write scary stories about hypothetical weapons. This science fiction game is not played for fun. It is played for money." Knowing this highly-sophisticated system of oppression benefits the few who *have* at the expense of the many who *ain't got,* and witnessing its roots in the exploitation of poor and working people of color, what is our recourse? How do we overcome the descendants of Goliath and topple Rome's great-grandchild? One answer, curiously enough, starts from a very simple and, for some, an unlikely place. Love.

> *"At the risk of sounding ridiculous, I say all true revolutionaries are guided by great feelings of love."*
>
> -Che Guevera

Not the stuff of melodramatic romance or government sex scandals, but an engaged praxis-based Love. A Love which operates within individuals, interpersonal relationships, and reaches our local and global communities. For as Che observes, Love is the most revolutionary act anyone subverting white supremacist patriarchal capitalism can commit. Self-love is the ultimate crime against a hedonistic corporate America which profits daily from the promotion of loveless individualism. This neo-capitalist system is sustained by commodity fetishism and the impulse to possess.

This impulse to possess suffocates Love. It destructively erodes our relationship to love from organic interactions to utility-based, opportunity cost exchanges. The compulsion to possess material objects and translate that practice into social interaction is the central ritual of a dying way of life. Love takes no prisoners, because, as Kahlil Gibran famously prophesied, it cannot be possessed and does not possess. That is the work of fear. "For what are your possessions? But things you keep for fear you may need them tomorrow?"

The possession, trapping, confinement, owning of "things" easily transforms into the possession, trapping, confining, and owning of people. Consequently, the prison industrial complex in the U.S. is the offspring of the transatlantic slave trade. Yes, prisons are, in fact, modern day slavery. The mural passed each day by incarcerated high school students, 16-19 years old, as they walk down the long grey hallway of Rikers Island Academy, features an image unlike anything we'd ever witnessed in an "educational" setting. A male figure, crouched down on one knee, appears divided into two halves. His back half appears in a green prison jump suit. His front half wears the green fatigues of a soldier at war and aims his assault rifle at an unseen target. The caption over the split figure reads: "choose your green."

Is the only place for black, brown, working and poor youth in America on the battlefield or behind bars? The promise of experiencing death-- either of the spirit for those confined behind bars, or a physical death for those on battlefields -- are the only future prospects offered to these imprisoned youth. Where is the hope for a life inspired and informed by love behind the barbed wire through which they witness planes taking off from LaGuardia airport, less than 100 yards away, each and every day?

What suggests the decline of human civilization more than the absence of love?

Yet this is rapidly becoming the hallmark of our fear-based society. Mainstream media conglomerates conspire with government officials invested in wars on terror and drugs and niggers of every color, class and caste. They instill fear in our consciousness on the
daily. Stereotypical stories, playing on this manufactured fear, invade our flat and silver screens, and hollyweird portrayals hijack our rationality by boxing groups of people into one villainous archetype. An Arab man will fly a plane into western metropolitan skyscrapers or suicide bomb public transportation vehicles. A black teenager will sell drugs to a crack-addicted mother or steal a white woman's purse.

Fear is innately confining. Corporate interests are deeply invested in selling us these "things" to profit from our fears. Weather on alarm systems or weapons systems, over the counter pills or paramilitary riot gear, spend some more money and ease away your anxiety-related-paranoia-hysteria by safekeeping your possessions at the expense of your sanity. The corporate design of fear is emblazoned onto bars, embedded into fences, etched into walls and evident in reluctant eye contact. bell hooks exposes that our "...cultural emphasis on endless consumption deflects attention from spiritual hunger."

Love, on the other hand, is pouring, effusive. There are no bars for Love, because Love is tantamount to liberation. The search for love requires letting go of fear. This is where love and fear are linked. In a nation daily reminded of questionable threats to national security and color-coded causes for us to live in fear of our neighbor, is there any person who is undeserving of love? Neither the Bible, Torah, Quran nor the Bhagavad Gita embraces a "three strikes" policy for Love. If Love involves forgiveness, reconciliation and reparation, there should be no disenfranchisement of formerly incarcerated people, no restriction of financial aid from college, no social stigma for a non-violent offense, and no record of egregious human rights violations for those in American prisons.

> *"Seriously, I remember I was 7 when rap came mysteriously and made me feel 11. It understood me and made my ghetto heaven I understood it as the new poor people's weapon."*
>
> -K'Naan

Art is an instrument for social change because in its conception and performance it requires actively engaging the love of the individual and the community. As Love implodes edifices of fear, the possibility for transformation rises from its ashes.

This is the work Lyrics on Lockdown urges with its philosophy rooted in creative and critical literacies. On any given day, in a classroom of teens incarcerated on Rikers Island, and college/graduate students from Columbia, NYU or the New School University, you can join in a Frerie-inspired lesson plan linking Cassidy, Dead Prez, Omali Yeshitela and Immortal Technique to deconstruct the hustling game from the streets of Brooklyn to the shores of Peru. From Assata Shakur's inspiring personal story, to Augusto Boal's interactive theatre games and participatory workshop performance style, from Tupac Shakur's "Thug Life" code to Noam Chomsky's analysis of mainstream corporate media's investment in manufacturing consent, LOL workshops, performances and lesson plans courageously link an extraordinary range of sources not only to address human rights violations on the block and behind bars, but also the value and power of our common humanity. This expansive scope is reflected in the poetry and prose of this anthology.

For bell hooks, "love and healing are acts of political resistance." With this in mind, it is no surprise the LOL campaign first emerged as an outgrowth of letters written by ex-Black Panther and Black Liberation Army activist Jalil Abdul Muntaqim. After spending more than three decades in prison for a crime he did not commit, Jalil wrote a founding member of Blackout Arts Collective in response to an article he'd written about being racially profiled and wrongfully incarcerated in his second year at Harvard Law. That elder's urgent request, for a university student to utilize his position of relative privilege to organize artists, activists, and educators to raise awareness and mobilize resistance to the prison crisis in America, was the seed that sprouted into this national movement.

Such a movement would be meaningless without engaging those most directly impacted by its human rights violations. And so, for five years beginning in 2001, the Lyrics on Lockdown tour reached correctional facilities, community venues and colleges in 25 states nationwide during an annual summer tour featuring performances and workshops by hip hop, spoken word, theater, dance and visual artists, activists and educators whose work addresses the realities of the prison industrial complex.

With the training, networks and solidarity of organizations like the Malcolm X Grassroots Movement, Prison Moratorium Project, Ella Baker Center for Human Rights, Critical Resistance, AFSC and OSI, the tour affected the consciousness of millions. With the critical visionary support of individuals like wrongly convicted poet prison activist Nanon Williams and voting rights legal scholar-activist Lani Guinier, the campaign has been incorporated into the curriculum of colleges and correctional facilities throughout the nation and continues to grow in depth and scope.

> *"The ink of a scholar is worth a thousand times more than the blood of a martyr."*
>
> -Lupe Fiasco
> (reciting an oft-quote saying of Prophet Muhammad PBUH).

For Jeff, a teenager with a "C" trailing him like a second shadow to re-imagine himself as an inspired, intelligent human being as deserving of life and love as anyone else, is truly transformative. For this young man written off by classrooms and courtrooms to counter social stigmas and inequities by writing himself back into a future rich with possibilities beyond the material poverty of the environment into which he was born, that is, without a doubt, revolutionary. The next generation is writing its own future by beating back the penitentiary with the pen and the pad, and reclaiming the power of love over fear.

Sourcebook of criminal justice statistics Online,
http://www.albany.edu/sourcebook/pdf/t2362007.pdf

Information compiled from Prison Moratorium Project "Prison Industrial Complex: The Critical Breakdown" fact sheet.

"The Fear Industry" by Alan Reynolds, Washington Times, May 6, 2007,
http://www3.washingtontimes.com/commentary/20070505-101330-9891r.htm

hooks, bell, *all about love: new visions*. New York Harper Perennial, 2000, p.72.

"Ingredients of Love," interview by Juniper Glass, Ascent magazine,
http://www.ascentmagazine.com/articles.aspx?articleID=133&issueID=24

POVERTY IS A MOTHER

by Bryonn Bain

Poverty spoke to her sons
loaded up both their guns saying
get blueprints for the white house and the crack house
study plans to the pentagon and the projects inside out

Infiltrate the estate of the greedy
take back or burn whatever they didn't earn
then return what rightfully belongs to the needy
feed your babies daily and then come back to see me

Poverty raised some bad ass boys
armed to the hungry teeth to bring the noise
brothers who live and love to beef for their beliefs
but mama can't let them be divided and destroyed

So Poverty speaks to her boys saying...
> *Study your weapons as well as your words*
> *Master the art of war and the science of herbs*

Analyze Angela Davis, build on Fanon, break down Marx
never blow up a building and leave behind identifying marks

So goes the list some dub terrorist
Poverty: part bank robber part black power fist
got pimps and panthers serving time together
freedom fighters and felons rebelling since forever

Poverty ain't hard to see
pregnant with Liberation and Larceny
breast feeding Uprising and Armed Robbery
on that mother's milk raised my brother and me

Poverty mothered us just fine
Our government names? *Revolution & Crime*
them bad ass kids acting up all the damn time
everything but obeying the king on they law defying minds

Revolution and Crime
You know my brother and I
them niggas who love to get out of line
crashed auction block parties and drop bad cops like a dime
don't run tell mama I done lost my mind
was you at the back of that welfare-healthcare-don't care line?
You try single handedly raising niggas like Revolution & Crime
deadbeat daddy out televising lies justify genocide far and wide
poisoning sub-Saharan tribes so seeds can't breathe
Morphing Aztec queens into morphine fiends

Wealth is who the man claims to be
some call him Uncle Sam but see
Greed is who he is to me

No payback for Native lands jacked in his new world slaughter
Greed gives thanks for the day he took away our borders
turns indigenous holocaust into a holiday
Celebrates the rape of native daughtersc

Greed pays Propaganda to silence Rage
strangles Consciousness in every age
but Poverty raised us to misbehave
raise hell until we kiss the grave

Poverty is the mother of Revolution and Crime

Them bad ass kids acting up all the damn time
them niggas who love to get out of line
everything but obeying the king
on our law defying minds
Mama raised us to misbehave

Raise hell until we kiss the grave
said we got to break these chains of ours
quit picking cotton and cutting cane for cowards
you better riot with your hammer and a hidden camera
saw off that shotgun to break Assata out the slammer
reprogram old man Sam's geopolitical grammar

Bed-Stuy to Baghdad and Harlem to Havana

Study your weapons as well as your words
Master the art of war and the science of herbs

Analyze Angela Davis, build on Fanon, break down Marx
Never blow up a building and leave behind identifying marks

Understand overstand innerstand
The plans of the pentagon and the projects inside out
Get blueprints for the white house and the crack house
Study plans to the pentagon and the projects inside out

Infiltrate the estate of the greedy
Take back or burn whatever they didn't earn
Then return what rightfully belongs to the needy
Feed your babies daily and then come back to see me

Poverty. Mother of Revolution and Crime

Them bad ass kids acting up all the damn time
Them niggas who love to get out of line
Everything but obeying the king
On our law defying minds

No time to blame men with no shame
No time to lick shots without aim
No time for slackness
Only change
Let no man call mama out her name

Time to change mama's name
Change mama's name
Change mama's name
Back to

On Society... On Jail...

How much different is this from slavery.

When we get chained and pushed around, **this is bullshit!**
You got to be gaming me.

When I'm **pushed inside a cell** and expected to act *civilized.*
Being tortured, locked in all days. Is that the best way
you thought will help me realize.
I think that you're the ones that need to see, that everybody
your doing this to is everyone who looks like me.

And you look at the color of my skin and you tell me

This is not slavery.

GUIDELINES:

At the beginning of each workshop series, the guidelines to shape each following workshop are created together as a group, as a form of social contract. It is important that all participate in the creation of guidelines, and that guidelines are reviewed at the beginning of each workshop. Below is a sample of guidelines agreed upon by the most recent series of workshops facilitated by New School students. They suggested that everyone participating in the workshop tag his/her signature on the easel paper surrounding their agreement.

1. One Mic

2. Respect Other's Opinions

3. Respect Other's Work

4. Be Honest, Keep it Real

5. Ago, Ame

6. Be Yourself - No Swagga- Jackin'

7. Give 100%

Love

...has *no compassion*,

when you're in love it feels

$\qquad\qquad\qquad\qquad$ like imagining.

$\qquad\qquad$ The setting sun colors of orange + red.

$\qquad\qquad\qquad\qquad$ You love others.
$\qquad\qquad\qquad$ If you do what you gotta do.

X ray vision sees through the masks.

To make love. To love what is.

I LOVE YOU

Love is *trust*

Love is a bond

Love is loyalty

Love is everything

I love people that jump out the window for me
So I jump out the window for them
Love has no capacity
But when you're in love it feels like
You're imagining

WHAT IS LOVE: One night I was walking to the store with a gun on me when I saw this girl I used to mess with. And this cop was rolling around the block, looking hard into my face. So I told the girl I used to mess with, can she put the gun I had on me in her purse and go home? And she did it. Right then the cop pulled me over and started pat frisking me. They didn't find the gun cause my girl walked home with it. Now that is love, because I could have went down if she didn't hold it for me.

In my life, love has no limit
Are you in love if you sleep with all these
different types of women?
Love should be faithful

Push your love to the limit
This person might be the one raising your children
You say that he or she is your heart
but you beat them and leave nothing but marks?

He or she is the sun and you are the moon
Without them you live in a dark lagoon
You show them how far your love goes
You give them your life and your soul.

Yo love, what's good yo?

I'm chillin...maintaining...

Yo love, you love me so much...

Why don't you get me the fuck out of here!?

The world is as round as a handball,

so like a clock tower,

likewise I stand **tall.**

I ROAR with horsepower just like an engine.

It's like a dog-versus-turtle in a race, I will win.

My life is like milk on the table for days, it is spoilt.

Love is like butter to me, it slips away like oil.

Time

is hard to catch up to,

like a man chasing a car on foot

when he knows he's through.

Dashawn
March 26, 2004

If my father was ever there for me

I think I might have had a better

chance of staying away from jail,

and I might have been different altogether.

I think I could have had less love for the streetz,

and spent more time looking up to my pops.

From my experience, I learned

when I have kids to tell them not

to make the same mistakes.

I won't say my brothers or friends

are responsible for how I ended up.

It's just me being me.

Well I'm writing this letter while I'm locked up
and let me start by telling you
that I was locked up plenty of times before
I wrote this letter, but it wasn't serious.
But about men, please don't get involved
with them they're a real problem.

Why-because all they do is fuck
different girls all day
and you might not know what those men have
they might have HIV or AIDS
and you don't want that.
Another thing you don't want
to end up in the streets
because a lot of bad things could happen
while you by yourself
people get involved in drugs and prostitution

I don't want that for u,
I want the best.

Another thing is don't use drugs...
it's not good to be a druggie
listen to your Mom and don't give her a hard problem
She don't need all that stress
she already have ya 3 to deal with.

I have a good sense of humor.

I have dreams

> to marry my girl,
>
> take care of my daughters,
>
> and to further my education
>
> in order to support my girl.

To be free...

LET PEOPLE KNOW WHAT IT MEANS TO BE FREE...

> You don't appreciate what you have until you are locked up.

I have a generous spirit...

> *I love food.*

One day

        I was playing basketball and ***the old head niggas***

            kick us off the court so they can play

              but they didn't have enough people

      so they pick me and I was doing what I do best

and from then on I got to play wit them and I got better as time past!

                                        RESPECT!

Gender is taboo on Riker's Island

precisely because of how important and personal it is.

Living in an all-male space

creates a particular atmosphere of masculinity

virtually unparalleled in any other space;

but prison's articulation of what being a "man" is cannot exist

without the creation of a compatible idea of what being a "woman" is.

The elision of girls and women from the new community at Rikers

forced new evaluation of how we (Columbia and Rikers students alike)

came to learn our gendered versions of identity—

that is, our collective ideas

on the roles that men play in women's lives

and that women play in men's lives.

1. In order to be a man you have to take full responsibility about what you do, and act mature.

2. Being a man in jail is never sending it in, and fighting for your respect to stay out of trouble.

3. I learned to be a man from my brother when I was growing up with him.

4. My brother had a street life, a rough life selling drugs, getting his weight up, and straight getting money.

Instead of saying...

skeezer
ho
bitch
chickenhead
slid
slut
project ho
bird
pigeon
2 dollar ho
ski
skeet
ho

We can call our *sisters*...

The Constitution of Mapi-Life-Tail

"The Future"
Each week, students participated in a different workshop focusing around various issues ranging from social liberation, to personal freedom, the prison system, family, life at Rikers, or any other subject the students were interested in discussing. The following is the conclusion of one workshop where students were asked to think about what people need to survive, and how different people can survive together. They divided into three groups, which each created three possible "societies" based on wants, needs, education, and other social structures. These three groups then came together and combined the wants and needs of everyone into a single society. All comments and suggestions made by the students are included here.

Goal: Create a culture. Design your own class structure, government, and police and military (if any apply).

This will help to understand:
    how to live with others,
    the importance of communication,
    culture reversal roles,
    special days (i.e. holidays),
    the foundations of social structures.

Challenge: Due to a global disaster, three separate societies have been in search of land suitable for sustaining life. They all arrive at the last piece of land on earth. They must work out their differences, and come together to form one society.

Here are the results:

Society 1: Papis and Mamis= Mapi

What are their Wants & Needs?
Water
Freedom
Land to grow food
Animals for breeding
Bank (money)
Materials (clothes, etc.)
Power

Education System?
Schools
Only our society is educated
Scientists

What Laws are Important?
No cops (because they don't fight for their country)
Army (to enforce the law)
Maytags (soldiers=slaves)
No jails
No gangs
Our language is the official language of the land

What is the Religion?
Respect the "FAN" or get chopped up
No gays

Society 2: Freedom and Life

What are their Wants & Needs?
Oil
Money
Marijuana
Buildings
Houses

Education System?
Teachers
Loans for higher education

What Laws are Important?
Military (for protection)
Security in every domain
Freedom of speech
Prisons
Rehabilitation
(for non violent offenders)
No adolescents locked up

Jobs?
Minimum starting salary
                ($30,000)
Police
Cosmetologists
Doctors
Architects

What is the Government System?
Organized structural-economics/political
Urgent medical care is free

Society 3: The People of the Island of Blacktail

What are their Wants & Needs?
Water
Crops
No clothes
Animals (no vegetarians)
Wood
Gas
Boats & Canoes
Houses

Education System?
No taxes
No jobs: but everyone has a designated task
No race: everybody brown
Marijuana
Entertainment (music/dance)

What Laws are Important?
No rules: they will be developed when problems arise
Women cook
Rocks/Weapons to hurt; no killing amongst ourselves
Trade system

What is the Religion?
No gays (applies to male on male sex)
Sex (free love)
Loving nature
No sexually transmitted diseases
Appreciate everything

The Constitution of Mapi-Life-Tail

This document represents the combination of the three societies that the students agreed upon when they came together. The name of the newly formed society is derived from parts of the names of each former society. Very little was agreed upon between the three societies. We can only speculate as to what progress would have been made in future meetings.

Name of New Land: Mapi-Life-Tail
Language: Mapi
Religion: Free to worship whatever GOD they want
Law: Men must wear clothes - women are nude

Gary

Weeks go by while my life is bad
and my feeling ● will cry

abnormal

communication

~~Sensitive~~

president

◄ area

Conception
18 18
5   8 8 8

The things that remind me of **HOME.**

Home is a place where there is *NO shit on the floor.*

Where you hear **gunshots**
                                                and everybody hit the floor.

Home *is a place where you could just* **chill.**

        A place where your family come.

Home *is a place where* **my family loves me.**

        A place where everybody's good and things are funny.

Home *is a place where* **I feel safe.**

        But sometimes you got to worry about getting chased by jakes.

I walk down my **block.**
see nothing but black faces like mine.
see dudes on the corner
doin the same thing they was doin when I left
but I ain't stressing it.
*I don't look down on them
cause they doin what they got
to do to survive*

                                            Young boys actin a fool
on the block cause their moms & pops
is at work and there is no one
to look after them
i can't down their parents cause
they just doin *what they got to do to survive*
how can i fault these cats when
they are just products of a society
where

before they were born they were already public enemy #1

*where before they were born
society had already had em
pictured holding a gun*

so when i look
into the eyes of these boys
i see the hate
their shoulders HUNCHED
over from the weight
of society's oppression

i see the girls
who run around
in short skirts letting
guys touch them cause

they grew up in a society where

the only important

thing on them is

THEIR ASS AND WHAT'S

BETWEEN THEIR LEGS

i grew up
in this society
was born and raised
people moved in
people moved out
but the fucked up
thing is that it still
hasn't changed

The streets of the city
concrete, cold, and dirty
straight out of the
sticky summer, gutter smelly
buildings as high as the sky
crowded trains, screeching tracks that cry.
The motion and commotion
of people constantly
in a rush, fast paced
always moving.
Somewhere in between the bridge
and blocks is me.
At home whatever that may be.
Home sweet home is expression
I never cared to speak.
In the tumbling, thundering noise
In home from the streets
this city never does sleep.
This morning rush bursts with
their morning coffee
Blood shot eyes with greed
you'd think the city was on speed
Passing bystanders, passing people
too busy, passin' by me.
But where are all you going?
We got the whole night
In this city that
never sleeps.

Born. Struggle. Life. Smiles. Tears.
I got needs. I didn't understand. Only feared.
No one told me how to live, how to give.
No one showed me where was home. Left alone.
Escape from the outside. Shut away the inside.
Run away from anything, everything. All of me.
Out of my skin. Wash away the sin.
Where is home? I don't know. Where to go.
Home. I've got nothing to show.
Left alone. Just me and my bones.
Kept on looking. Searching for the fake.
It was a mistake. I didn't know. I didn't know
Where to find home. Still here, nothin's changed.
Home. And here I am. Still alone. Just rearranged.
Home. Nothing to show. Except home.
Right here. Right now. In my bones
Home. Home. I found it.
In my heart. In my soul. Home.
Here I am home.

Bein' home is where I want to be.
Smoking trees settin' hush like I'm supposed to be.
Seein' niggas on the corner hustling day and night
wit the thought of makin' money is just something I like,
lookin' at the ladies walk by so I can try to holla
not knowin' that she thinking that I aint got a dolla.
Wit an ass like delicious her head game is vicious.
Thinking just because she went down that I'ma get the lickin'.
We got c-buns and some dummies. Some high-class junkies.
And they will do anything for a hit and some money.
Transactions in the buildings where the friends get the chillin',
if they short up on the money then there's gonna be some killin'.
When you livin' like a villin and not thinkin' about ur family or ur
children. It's the hood we call home. Because that's where our heart is
and if we take it away that's when we become life less.
So look at me and what u see, I'm facing 26 to life
and home is where I wanna be.

The streets is where I was raised. I live at home with my mom but I was too busy in the streets selling drugs that she missed me at home for a couple of days. The days I didn't come home my mother wondered if her only son would ever make it back home. She would call me on the phone to see if I'm alright and staying out of trouble. I said *YEAH* knowing damn well I'm out doing wrong. Following after what I saw older niggas do made me think about dropping out of school which I knew people would consider me a fool. It really didn't matter to me cause I had to do what I had to do to survive on the streets, it went from just packing the heat to knocking niggas off their feet. *You gotta do what you gotta do.* From me doing wrong look at me now, **I'm locked up trying to fucking sing a song about home.**

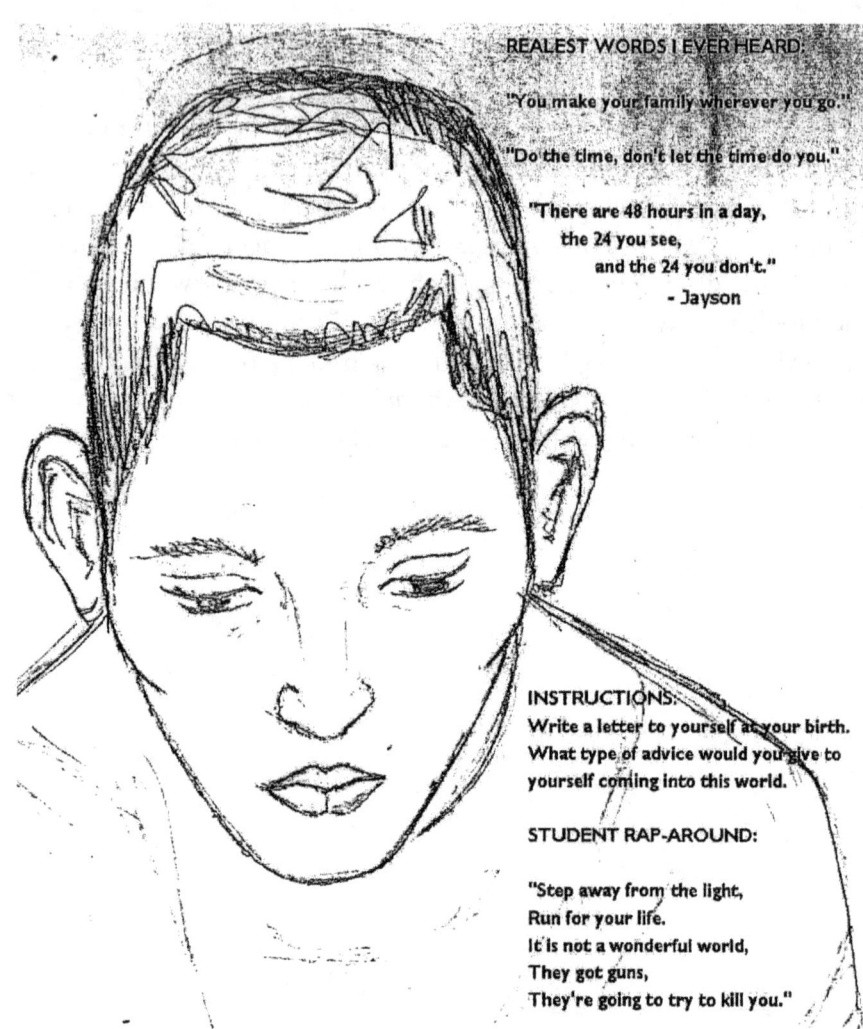

REALEST WORDS I EVER HEARD:

"You make your family wherever you go."

"Do the time, don't let the time do you."

"There are 48 hours in a day,
the 24 you see,
and the 24 you don't."
     - Jayson

INSTRUCTIONS:
Write a letter to yourself at your birth. What type of advice would you give to yourself coming into this world.

STUDENT RAP-AROUND:

"Step away from the light,
Run for your life.
It is not a wonderful world,
They got guns,
They're going to try to kill you."

My home is with my friends in Brownsville.

I was raised on the playground where I spent my days

chillin out maxin after school

hangin w/ my boys and my girls too.

Going to a party hang out there

cops come thru the crib, people running

out the back cause they're here.

I'm looking around like what should I do

Should I turn myself in or should

I run away too

Times is hard. Times is deep.

Tryin to get away from the police.

Tryin to get home. Tryin to get to my house.

So I can relax on my couch.

Now I'm home, now I'm peaceful

tryin to get sleep so I can see you.

Wake up in the morning, see my friends

So we can talk about the night,

then do it all again.

Home is a place you go to for family
For that feeling of security. That never really did it for me.
A comfortable cage, lined with carpets and couches.
I used to feel secure, but now that's where my doubt lives.
I doubt I can live in one place for too long.
I doubt I can articulate my thoughts in this song.
It's like being alone is the way to be here,
The second you let someone in, you bow to their needs
And life is too short, to live for somebody else,
If the ships going under, we should all save ourselves.
But isn't that the thinking that's ruined our society?
Why do I think in ideals but live with hypocrisy?
Should I feel sorry that a home to me
is the voice in my head that says what I need,
and if I need to get away from your suburban dream,
and so selfishly retreat to my own inner journey,
Don't be offended. My life hasn't ended. I'm just
Doing some time before I am confined.

Born n raised in BK seen what hell looks like.
Life of a hustler, games of a gambler,
loved by few, hated by many, respected by all.
Family loved me. Fam/streets raised me
locked up living in a hell-hole chased by cops
duck them shots playing the cards I was dealt.
Trying to build but taking this shit the streets brought
waking up in cold sweats day by day wondering
if it was my time to go
cause at the rate I was going I didn't know
cold hearted to some loveable to few.
Pops died. Me n my bothers cried.
Left in the dark thinking sometimes where is my heart.
Lost two brothers lost two sisters.
Watched my nigga die, tears in his eyes, blood in his mouth,
screaming out Y!

you lose me, and

        I take you along
        packed up tightly in my insides
        home-cooked

you leak from me

        in sweaty armpits and fists
        when I'm forced to go back, and bring forth

Home held me like groceries in rain

        fingers turning white and numb
        frigid from cold, refusing to let go
        my house being sold
        if Dad's mind can't hold
        got no home to go back to
        only enough reserves to sweat

I thought I had it all planned

> in my journey through life
> hustling on the street corners n breaking night
> making fast money but what was it all worth
> addicted to the streets I think I've been cursed
> dreams of getting rich and going legit
> but all I seen in my future is this jail shit

I'm lost I'm trying to find my path

> every time I get close I'm lured by a demon called cash
> how long will this battle of good n evil in me last? I don't know
> But what I do know is I have to make this choice past
> cause time seems like is going in a flash

I NEED TO REALIZE THAT LIFE IN THE STREETS

ISN'T ALL I HAVE.

bone stacked on bone
with liquid running thru it
forms the frame that keeps me
to see the world and keep me through.

one end running towards the ground
the other heading skyward
keeps me balanced on a spinning earth
that tries to throw me off.

i keep walking, walking forward
heel hitting ground and lifting
words come at me back again
and so i'm always sifting.

searching for the truth
the spine in every lie
reaching out to feel those messy bumbs
that keeps me asking why.

why i stand in this room speaking now
or where my family's from
why healing takes so long
and when is change gonna come?

if you get to the heart of the matter
it's easier to see where people are coming from
the fire that burns each day bright
makes muscles move
find our way in the night.

i put my ear to the ground to listen
for bold hearts beating
coz whatever earth i stand on
i know that someone's breathing.

sometimes it's a fight to stay alive
and my pulse feels like a hammer
marking time or breaking walls down
that's the choice i have to make.

every place has got a rhythm
it just takes some time to hear it
settle down onto my knees
so i can really feel it.

The truth *is something that most people don't tell.* The truth sometimes sets some away from hell. The truth is not something that always sets you free. Just being true to yourself shows who we are. The truth is knowing that you did wrong and admit your mistakes. But sometimes the truth doesn't want to be heard so we get sent away. Truth is showing that you are not scared and when its told some people feel fear. The truth gains trust and sometimes we don't want to tell the truth we must. We tell the truth to ourselves, but with everybody else the truth is something held.

Who do I tell the truth to besides me?

I'll tell the truth to you, only if you tell the truth to me.
That's why they say the truth sets us free.

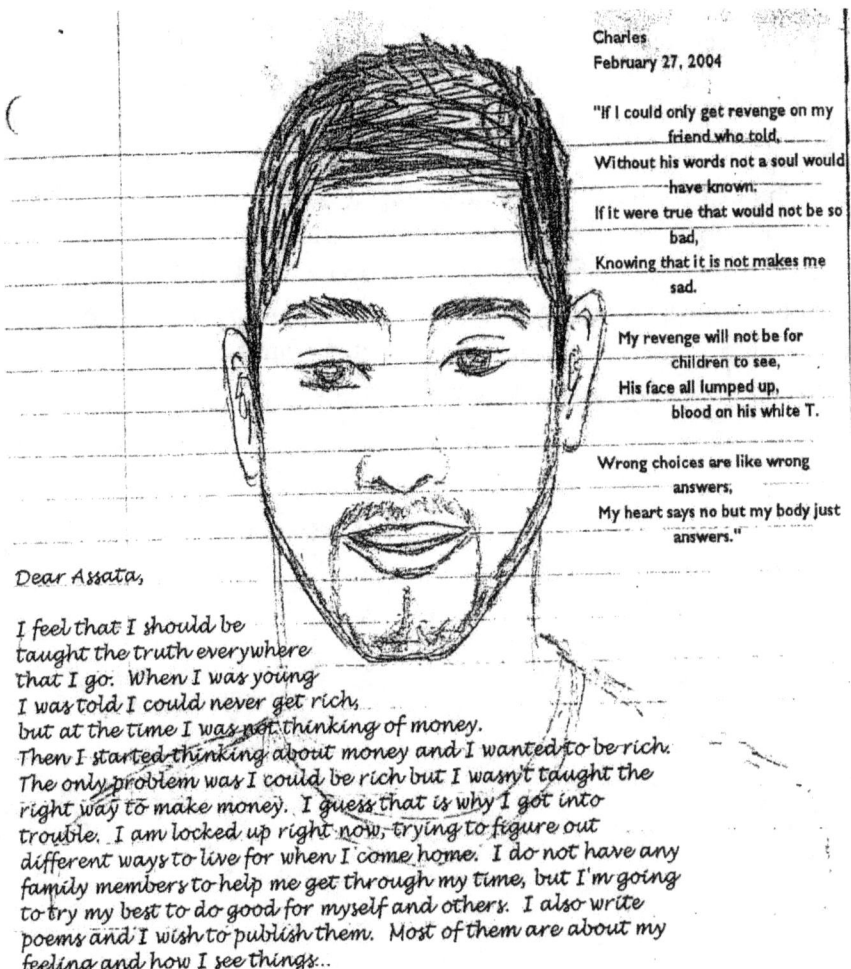

Charles
February 27, 2004

"If I could only get revenge on my friend who told,
Without his words not a soul would have known.
If it were true that would not be so bad,
Knowing that it is not makes me sad.
My revenge will not be for children to see,
His face all lumped up,
blood on his white T.
Wrong choices are like wrong answers,
My heart says no but my body just answers."

Dear Assata,

I feel that I should be taught the truth everywhere that I go. When I was young I was told I could never get rich, but at the time I was not thinking of money. Then I started thinking about money and I wanted to be rich. The only problem was I could be rich but I wasn't taught the right way to make money. I guess that is why I got into trouble. I am locked up right now, trying to figure out different ways to live for when I come home. I do not have any family members to help me get through my time, but I'm going to try my best to do good for myself and others. I also write poems and I wish to publish them. Most of them are about my feeling and how I see things...

Charles

I feel that I should be taught the truth everywhere that I go. When I was young I was told I could never get rich, but at the time I was thinking of money. Then I started thinking about money and I wanted to be rich. The only problem was I could be rich but I wasn't taught the right way to make money. I guess that is why I got into trouble. I am locked up right now, trying to figure out different ways to live for when I come home. I do not have any family members to help me get through my time, but I'm going to try my best to do good for myself, and others. I also write poems and I wish to publish them. Most of them are about my feelings and how I see things.

*If you can lie to yourself, you can lie to anybody,
you're not trustworthy.*

To me **hip hop** means A *music*
based on rhyming no matter
if its fiction or reality. **hip hop**
can be ANGER, love, *scared,* it can
be a lot its all on what u talk about.

Hip hop means you have
a very special talent which is music

HIP HOP CAN CHANGE

SOMEONE'S WHOLE LIFE AROUND

With hip hop
u can be poor one day
and rich the next

hip hop has a lot of power
believe it or not.

You can
basically talk about anything no
matter whats the scenario long
as it sounds good or makes
a little bit of sense we will be good.
To go hip hop is live it's a performance
its also something that can be watched by someone else.

I love hip hop.

Hip Hop means
new way of eXpress your self. A way of
hiding the pain, pain... a way of tellin
somebody your feelings. Hip Hop is
a growing Movement its not a white or
Black thing. It's a way of life. No fighting no killin
Just music or poems and dancing
Having fun Hip Hop means,
to me. Lyrics flow punch line rhythm melody.

Hip hop means everything to me, if I never had it how would I feel. I wouldn't be able to chant, pickup my hands & do the boogz. There wouldn't be JayZ, Fab or Weezy to boost my mood when I feel down. There wouldn't be a Run DMC or a Slick Rick to tell me the past of hip hop. When I listen to hip hop its like energizer to the bunny because I keep going once I can get it. If there was no T-pain I would have to work up more courage to by her a drink or make up my own notion of a Shawty. Hip-hop is my world even though its changed, New-rappers & artists but its still the same game. Who's album will sell more the million$ of fans. Im not sure about the other 999,000 but I know im one.

To me hip-hop means to rap to freestyle to
be nice to be wack to spit crack to fix that
to flip that pack to rewind an redo all of that.
I rap because im nice, I know how to fight,
play alright.

To me hip hop means a group of words that mean
a lot to ones who listen, for the ones who don't lose
a lot of lesson an blessin. You could rap an get
rich spit a lot of hot shit, that could get
flip. Leave you with a brick.

To me hip hop means express
wat you feel feel feel hip hop
means real life drama confusion
hip hop means drugs
raps --- thugs hip hop
can mean a lot of things
freedom peace --- hip hop
means me love family ---
transformance/art/hip
hop means culture.

Without hip hop there's no truth.

hip hop is
messin with the minds
of kids
memorizing lines
imagining crimes
mimicking styles

*this is not what hip hop
was but is*

dropping false knowledge
what happiness is
what success looks like
confusing money with bliss
replacing **REALNESS**
with this:

*make it rain on them hoes
get those nice clothes
get that escalade
even though you don't have a home
disrespect your women
till they let you
cause they got nowhere
else to go
replace the flow
with hooks to make
you wiggle
go girl go
go get that money
go get that dough*

go till you have no place to go

DEAR OBAMA,

we gotta problem
and it's nothing to do with your name
sounding like Osama

See our
nation's under siege
by a clandestine enemy
in the form of harsher sentencing
policies are threatening
Poisonous prejudices
vapors are setting in
The governments letting them
The media's spreading them
Racist cops are arresting them
I don't hear you stop
to protest for them

Comma
I don't mean to be a bother
I know there's two sides
of every problem
But there's a line
that you don't cross
when it comes to being human
or a monster
It's not something you started
and you were thinking about decriminalizing marijuana
but it's about the 13th Amendment
two million caged behind bars
and you can't let it go any farther

Obama,
crime is not a career choice
like a kid dreaming

of one day drug dealing
as he played with his toys

No,
It's a way to keep living
stuck in the situations people been given
Obama tell me how is
five years the minimum
for 500 grams of cocaine
add a little baking soda
and 5 grams crack will get you the same sentencing
How did our system come to that?

Look at the prisons their mostly brown and black
and when their released 70% of them go right back
No, it isn't a coincidence or bad luck
look up the stats online at prisonsucks

**NO, SLAVERY DIDN'T END LAST CENTURY
THEY JUST FREED SLAVES AND PUT THEM
IN THE PENITENTIARY**

Slow form of genocide on an ethnicity
with the war on drugs
but what about poverty
or the war against corporations
that exploit labor and hit the lottery
How about the war on racists?
They're allowed to protest and picket
while blacks are profiled by the way
they dress, talk, and live
Pac said *that's just the way it is*
once their booked, charged and raped as men
they're let out into the world again

A world that's not accepting
doesn't understand and

thinks it's fair what their getting
It's one vicious cycle
I bet you could guess the ending

Obama,
time spent in the pen
is meant to rehabilitate
Expand the mind and educate

There's no time to wait
There's no time to wait

                                                                                          But wait

They're
flushed out more dysfunctional
than when they came in
with their life
ripped right out from under them
Obama reevaluate the term incarceration
cause upon release date
there's no decarceration
You need to debrief them on their mental state
Crime charges should be swiped away
Give them their dignity and give back their name
Show them in society they have a place
Cause to lock up a problem
Doesn't mean it'll go away
Their hatred will grow into a quick tempered rage
The system has kicked them
to their knees
then kicked them out
and expect them to behave
Tell them
Go make good decisions
after you train them all how
to take detailed instructions
on what to do every single day

Why don't you cut off their hands
and tell them their only chance was to pray
this is the solution to make America feel safe

Obama,
FREEDOM IS NOT FREE
it comes with your 9 to 5
struggling to get by
Keep criminal short cuts
from that wondering eye
Cause three strikes
and there's nothing left for you or me
Wait, unless you got loads of money

But Obama,
I'm not asking you to shut down the prisons
in fact
expand them to the billions
change the signs to read "Psychology"
Put all the guards in with them
so everyone can open their minds
Let the molecules mix
and get the people
back to a healthy condition
Strive to get them home with conviction
Obama, do you hear them
Can you listen?
Cause if you want to live free
It's a die hard trying to get that money
kind of mission

For now,

From the people
trapped
in
this system

Letters To J

This is a collection of some of the questions that came up between me and one of the many amazing young men I met on Rikers Island, who I will call J; while I tried to address and answer all of J's questions, I encountered some difficulty in determining the right way to speak to some of his ideas. The fine line between being honest about my ideas and being overly didactic was at the center of most of the hesitation I sometimes felt while writing to J. I have always been completely honest with J, but I also want to be a source of friendship and support for him. Unwittingly using him as a depository for my ideas has been my biggest concern.

While I answered J in my letters to him exactly the same way that I answer him here, these responses incorporate more of my own stream of consciousness. In sharing these ideas and pieces of his letters, I hope to give an honest account of pieces of my experience developing a friendship outside of the classes.

*Everything in italics is directly quoted from J's letters.

Anonymous
3/15/04

I really think you and the others are full of knowledge and have a lot of wisdom to share with us young brothers on the inside.

These are times at Rikers when I need to know what is "knowledge", and what is it worth if I know I can't get you out of there. I don't know you well yet. This is the first letter I have received from you, and I already want you to destabilize whatever ideas you have about "knowledge" and "wisdom". I have never been a parent, teacher, or elder sibling, and I am scared of letting you down. I know I'm just a letter, or words in a letter. (at least I'm hand-writing it to you, getting away from the sterility of something called Times New Roman which looks nothing like an aesthetic version of how I think. I'm pretty sure that Times New Roman is beginning to affect the way I think and even imagine being able to write. If it is, that is just not right at all.) I don't want to inflate my role (if I even have one) in your (big, complicated, completely-foreign-to-me) life, but part of me needs to tell you there is not much "knowledge" or wisdom" for you from me. I can only tell you what I see in your situation, and I am banking on the idea that I might see something that you don't. The letters can't become cinematic. It's not fair to you or me.

-

I can honestly say I've lived a life of negativity... it seems like I always had bad luck.

I wonder whether self-worth is part of your emotional situation, and yet I hate the idea of my imposing some kind of naïve (semi-white) liberal lens onto my ideas about where you are coming from. What is a "life of negativity" to you, and what is positive?

Luck is such a tricky thing, J, most of the time it really is better called circumstance. I don't want to make you a representative of the PIC. I don't want to take the individual out of what you are saying to me. Bad luck doesn't mean anything to me. Luck is the grace of god, and luck is contingent, and luck is a myth at the same time. What is your circumstance?

-

What do you consider college to be, and what's the best part to you?

College is my circumstance, my "lucky", or rather my privileged circumstance. It is also my bourgeois ethic. It is also my south Asian guilt and my immigrant dream/psychic diasporas. College simultaneously unteaches and reinforces my own oppression. And yours. The best part is the good teachers. The best part is when I find an ideological kindred spirit. The best part is how sometimes I really believe that the currency here is ideas and not money or material goods. What would you think if I said the best part is how much "college" (and the institutions it works with) says I'm not supposed to see myself in you and you in me, but how much I already do?

3/29/04

I could honestly say that I always wanted a friend that represents a different kind of lifestyle, other than negativity and wrong doings.

There is that negativity again. What is it? What is negative? Why? I don't want to preach to you, J, I want you to set the tone for this relationship we are developing. What is wrongdoing and why is it wrong? You have no obligation to tell me why you are locked up, and yet I don't want to feed into your idea that what you did is unspeakable and necessarily even "wrong." I don't know yet. I'm not an arbitrator anyway. Why does class status lend some false notion of morality? In India, my dad always told me that the only people who were not corrupt were the poor. My father is romantic, I admit, but he is a humanizer of circumstance. When we are in India, I can tell he still sees people and not what the American in me sees-- circumstances, abject poverty, the evil of colonialism, racism, the World Bank all distilled into one moment of shanty town voyeurism. What is negative and what is wrong?

There, but for the grace of god, go I…

-

While in here my mother and dad are the only people I talk to besides you.

I want to be what you need me to be. When the boys at Rikers asked me whether I would ever like them, it was hard to dismiss them. It's not just an internalized gender oppression that makes me want to be pleasing, in a certain way, it's the recognition of the fact that on the outside you can ask for so much, and on the inside your brothers seem to need just the recognition of their humanness. Humanness: the ultimate reductive factor- I have never met a person that is bigger than human.

-

I feel I owe it to myself to see some different parts of the world, especially when there's my cousin (James) who dies in the only place he'd ever been.

I have a suspicion that the world is larger than anything I have ever considered. But my grandparents now live next to a Domino's pizza place. And I cried the second I saw the first McDonald's in Pune, where they lived, burger-free, my whole life. My dad told me not to cry because "all human creations end, even the Roman Empire ended, and who would have thought it ever would?" Maybe he is right, but just in case, let's try to see it all, my friend, before it gets any smaller.

-

I wrote this side of the letter after I saw you and the others leaving in which I watched you walk down the hall until I couldn't see you no more. The whole time just thinking how wonderful a person you are, and wishing there were more people in the world as wonderful as you are.

J., I think about you and the other brothers all the time. You will never know how true this is. You are the new lens through which I have started to try to interpret the world we live in. I am not "wonderful," I am incredibly human. I am still porous to the realities of the world and human truth and justice. When I leave Rikers, and you are looking at my back until you can't see me anymore, I am praying.

-

And I think its great that your Indian and study African American history, cause we all been through a struggle.

Tell it, brother, tell it. (I wish you could talk to a few of the people I've met along the way about this. You got it better than some of them, whether you realize that or not. I appreciate that, because that is a part of liberation to me.)

-

4/7/04

I didn't decide to not attend the last group session. I had to go to court. I don't have a problem with discussing revolution. I actually love the idea and the word alone.

I'm not judging your decision to come or not, Mouse. For one thing, you live through realities that I have never even seen. I love the idea of revolution too. What does your revolution look like? Can we build it together? Are we already?

My nephew is nine years of age, and he and I both like sports and music.

He is lucky to have you in his life.

-

I wish you the best and the enough.

What a wonderful concept "enough" is. I had a friend with a tattoo written in Nepali script, a Buddhist saying that translated to, "Love is All and I am Enough." What is "enough?" You and I are getting to know one another as time goes on. I was nervous about letting you down or boring you in the beginning. Now I feel that you and I have a real relationship. I still wish I knew, am I enough?

-

Happy birthday or belated. I hope you enjoyed it.

Thank you- I can't believe you remembered. How did you? I had dinner with my friends on my birthday; I wondered what you were doing when I was at dinner, because I was being lucid and thinking about thinking about what a "liberation birthday dinner" would look like. I wonder what you are doing right now.

-

4/21/04

It was really nice seeing you again, I enjoyed the session with the others as well.

When I see you, I forget that you are the same J. who writes these letters. Not because you seem to have different ideas, but because of the different atmospheres of space we share with each other, just you and I, and with all our other friends when we are together.

-

I think you and your friends hiking in Maine and sleeping in tents for a week is a very interesting experience.

Hiking is so white it almost makes me not like it. (Clearly those are my own issues.) J., I wish I could take you hiking. It creates such a different experience of the self and the collective from what we are used to in everyday life-- particularly urban life. I think there is a natural human sympathy for the outdoors.

Once Chris talked about liberation architecture, and how the ways that buildings are engineered reinforce types of oppressive power dynamics. I told Russell, Fernando, and Chris that in my vision of the architecture of a liberated space, there would be no walls-- maybe no buildings at all-- because walls, in and of themselves, privatize space. Maybe part of why I like hiking is that there are no walls, really. I wish I could take you hiking.

-

4/30/04

Today was our last day on Rikers. I am filled with sadness at the thought of never again seeing the majority of the brothers who have become such a welcome fixture to my week. There are three brothers who I have become most close with-- Kenny, Josh, and you. I am most sad about saying goodbye to you and Josh, because I am somehow certain that I will see Kenny again. I don't know whether I will see you again. Actually, I don't think I will. I am trying not to think about this, because goodbyes are very hard for me.

Going through security for the last time, I hate the yellow tags and I'm sick of the CO's joking, "Make sure you don't lose that, might take you a while to get back out!" Maybe I'm getting sensitive because it's the last day.

Fernando says that you are upset and do not want to join us. I go to talk to you. I'm surprised that the CO let me just walk into the dorm space. We talk for a while. Maybe 15 minutes. I don't want to ask you what went down that made you upset, because I can tell you are still upset about it and don't want to have to explain. Is it sad that I can't fully remember what we discussed? I only know that I tried not to focus on why you weren't coming.

When Laurent came in to check on us, it was one of the most "normal" human instances I will remember from Rikers: you were sitting on a bed, and I was sitting across from you on your bed. When Laurent walked in, just for a second, he reminded me of my dad coming into my bedroom to tell me that I had to go soon, and you remind me of a now nameless/faceless high school friend who stopped by to say hello. There was something so normal about it, considering the Riker's setting.

When we were done talking, and I was sufficiently convinced that there was no way you would come to the lesson, I stood up and tried to take my cinematic (at least the letters didn't get cinematic) last look at you. I remember being surprised that you were not as much taller than me as I had thought. I was pretty sure I'd never see you again, but that it was possible that you'd write to me. I hope you do. When I walked away, I was thinking that you must be watching me from the window for as long as you can until I disappear into a tiny dot. I was saying a prayer.

DEATH

When it came time to listen to *A Change is Gonna Come* by Sam Cooke and write about "struggle" and "hope," all of the students were very eager to share their work to a beat or acappella. The rhymes the students came up with on the dot were deep. They were real. The students were very encouraging of each other and urged college students to share their own work. I think all in all, we were best connected and focused this time.

I think the ground rules of respect, one mic, and self-determination sunk in.

STRUGGLE is the s p a c e

b/t a rock; a hard place

I done faced trials that've been hard to reconcile
what's important is to face it
not live life in denial
I'm my own judge
I put myself on trial
did I handle my b.s. or was I on some other shit?
gotta come out in the end
look in the mirror and know, I didn't give in
cave in for fake men

          I thug my issues
          I empower myself

bump all the distraction.
I keep that shit on the shelf

          I AM MY OWN HELP

but can't be scared to ask for help
live life well
I won't ever ring the bell
believe it

we all have the burden to say wrong when we see it,
we need change, it's time to be it

life goes on and time passes but I still feel regret,
I still feel pain and I'm angry with myself for never speaking up

struggle is the space between a rock and a hard place
I'm my own judge, I put myself on trial

work hard for what you want
nothing is given to you

surviving requires a heart beating
which won't happen if I'm not eating
be the food material—spiritual
I've got to get my fill.

It's a struggle to be locked up for somebody else's mistake.

Struggle pain dying in vain hustling on the street trynna get that money the man be posted on the bloc to running from the cop always trynna take wat you got in the middle of your life trynna make it to the top

S is 4 stamina

T is 4 tuff

R is 4 ruff

U is 4 us

G is 4 get it

G is 4 gold

L is 4 left

E is 4 except

Life is determined on how you live.
Life is something you have
but is not always going to be there
Life is something you could bring in this world.
Life is something that's not hard to create.

Life is something that some people waste.
Life is something easily taken as it is made.
Life is something that has been crazy for me.

Life is something you want to keep
so you have to think before you do.
Life is something easy to change depending on you be.
Life is something that can be taken from you so be careful
and watch what you do.

I can't ever stand without a helping hand.

The shadows seem deep, I can't ever sleep,

    My body feels weak.

I walk and sneak on to the mountain peaks,

    So high smoking weed

Makes my mouth too dry [for this man] to cry

Falling down

From my point of view I think these handouts stand for black people who believed in Civil Rights and equal rights and would not stop fighting for what they knew was right.

Today's street gangs are supposed to be fighting for pretty much the same thing. What I mean is that my group the "Bloods" originated from the Black Panthers so I pretty much understand what Black people are fighting for.

Looking out of a class, as the rain is falling softly, puttering
looking at the gray clouds, thinking over other Students muttering
thinking of how ironic it is that I'm in school and I'm in jail
thinking of how I want to succeed even though all else may fail.
What does God have in store for me?
What's my destination?
Am I supposed to wait this out or is what I'm doing procrastination?
When should the work begin since I've already been changed?
Am I even sane right now? Or am I just plain deranged?
Freedom over waters and freedom over chains,
a future full of losses and a future full of gains.
A future and freedom over lands and over seas,
why stay in jail and rot from self-loathing disease?
There's so much more out there than I even realize,
a lot more things to see with these here blue eyes.
All I seek is freedom; all I want is to succeed
Why live a life in bondage as if from freedom I secede?

I feel that people that got into trouble should get another chance.

Because if it's your first time maybe you'll learn your lesson.

If I had a second chance I know not to do things that I did.

Hopefully, I will get a second chance.

I want to finish high school. It's my last year, and **I only need 12 credits to finish**, then I don't know about college. I like school but I really don't want to go to college.

Hopefully, I could open my own business.

I want to be a businessman.

Maybe a Laundromat or something like that.

CALI
AKA
LIL TOOKIE

① Cultural Rights – (F)GRADE because we not being taught what we need to be taught jas-tar as about our role models that fought for us to live like how we live today. DR MARTIN LUTHER King, MALCOM X

② Right 2 Leisure Activity – I feel (A)GRADE that we have fun & can work out physically But At the same tyme to me I feel its still setting us up for failure cuz we in Jail getting bigger & we still young so as A male we try to compete with eachother causing problems cuz one feels stronger or bigger then the next man.

theres A white kid sitting next to me taking everything I said cuz he feel my swagg

There still got to be a prison in the world. Let's give them what they want. They want something that they can't have. Let's give them a job or something. Let's communicate with them. Let's learn what's their problem. Let's put them in a building for a couple of days and see what's their problem. You got a lot of people in the world with problems. Without a prison, where can they hold these individuals? If I was a counselor I'd sit down and talk to them. Help that person to the best ability. Give them family that can help him. But he's got to put effort in too. He has to put his mind to it. He has to get away from the street. I'd help him out if he came with me. If he felt like I'm helping him, he has to earn it. I'm not just going to give up on him. That's what a lot of people do. *You can't just give up on a guy and throw him back in the street.*

Slavery and Prison

We're locked down 24 hours.
We sleep and we eat.

They don't eat like the prisoners do.

We get guards.
We can't get privacy,
Just like slavery.
We got guards walking 24-7.

Where COs coming from,
if we do wrong we're getting hit,
Just like slavery.

Either way, we're still getting beaten.

They still got freedom,

We don't.

If somebody commit a crime,

I'll sit down, I'll talk to him.

I don't want my society to turn

just like you. I'll give him a job.

You got to earn it. If he don't want it,

I'll put him in a building or hospital—

not like prison, a program—

helping people with their problems.

The faster they move, the faster we move.

I write. All of the time. Every time I have a thought it goes on paper. I've been here for like nine months and I've been writing for nine months. *It doesn't help.* Frustration is too prevalent, too omnipotent for something as inanimate as writing. We need to rise. We need to go against the grain. We need to be a pain in the ass. The oppressor is an ass. Those who share our history, our ancestry, our skin color, our language, and interests, oppress us. It may be confusing, in that case, we need to figure shit out! We need to identify what it is that pisses us off and fight for it tooth and nail...

Take a punch to the face

burn your arm

cut your hand

get shot.

Boom, slash, bam, bbbrrehht

It washes over your body

Whatcha gonna do when the pain sets in

and your bleedin and heavin and just can't win

Gonna cry and run home or stand up tall

Whatcha gonna do with the pain-o

My advice to you is to stay out of jail.

There is nothing for you in here because

YOU WILL STARVE.

The food you're going to eat is
not good.

For example, you get
no salt on the food.

The food is dog food.

LOCKDOWN

Every week in class I come to the same alarming conclusion: *I have really been very privileged and very sheltered in my life so far.*

I always end up not understanding some of what is being said because on some level I cannot imagine life without certain aspects that I consider basic: good education, role models, encouragement, a safe home, etc. Every time that I am faced with the reality that not everyone grows up in an environment like I did makes me feel guilty. I feel guilty because I was given something that others were denied solely based on my skin color, my class, and my monetary standing. Basically, I feel guilty that I was lucky enough to be born into my fortune while others ended up with the short end of the stick. I thought that I had learned all that I could about these feelings in my college classroom, but I couldn't have been more wrong. It was not until I was in serious conversation with the men at Rikers High that I realized there are so many more levels to these feelings.

When many people think of prison, they think of metal bars, chains, inmates, violence, and retribution. One cannot imagine that this is only the beginning. There is no way to describe the realities of lockdown. The suffocation, the boredom, the waiting, and the cruelty are all elements that are forgotten; are all elements that don't seem to matter to the average person living on the outside. In our society there is the belief that if someone committed a crime they deserve to be locked-up. We say this because the word "criminal" is one of a crackhead, a thief, a rapist, and a murderer. It is a label of fear. It reduces a person to an animal who deserves to be caged. This label does not promote an image of hope, of struggle, or of resurrection.

There is a system in place where prisons are used to hide societal issues such as poverty and drug addiction, which relies on racism and patriarchy in order to function. There is a system in place that can only be described as modern-day slavery, with a societal stamp of approval. We use human sacrifice to believe that we are "tough on crime" with the imposition of legislation such as mandatory sentencing, three-strikes law, and sentence enhancement.

The PIC is an oppressive system that serves none: not victims, not "criminals," and not society. Prison seems like a solution, but it is not. It does not stop the fear, the nightmares, the self-hatred, the anger, or the resentment. Our justice system offers victims nothing other then a removed sense of justice, which does not serve justice or prevention, and least of all healing. Healing is a personal journey, and is the greatest level of neglect by our justice system. People are not systematic, and their pain and problems cannot be dealt with systematically. We are all offenders and victims. Our justice system needs to address why we are both, instead of making human sacrifices to the courts in hope that justice will be served. It simply does not work, and instead creates more victims.

It only takes being at Rikers Island for a minute for you to begin to feel the suffocating control symptomatic of a prison system that is specifically designed so that you become caught in its clutches and you lose your ability for free movement, space, and possibility. The freedom of choice is removed and the power of the system becomes supreme. If you are thinking to yourself that this is only true for the prisoners, you are mistaken. Anyone—inmates, correction officers, wardens, and yes visitors—who cross Rikers path lose his or her sense of freedom for the duration of the stay. The Prison Industrial Complex, once it gets its hand on you, will try to contain you for as long as it can. At every opportunity, the prison system will drain essential energy from you to feed its life source.

First off let me just say, when you arrive at Rikers, make sure you are prepared to wait. When our group from Columbia University pulled into the visitor's parking lot, we were told to wait for a van to come and get us to drive across the bridge that leads to one of New York's most infamous penal institutions. Guess what, the van never came. After a number of weeks of dialogue and clearances regarding our arrival, they had forgotten about us. After numerous phone calls down to the juvenile detention center, they had forgotten about us. There was only one option afforded to us. We took the public bus that the loved ones visiting inmates take.

Before leaving our van, we made sure to leave any personal items that may be confiscated or result in being denied access. That means no cell phones, no cameras, no keys, no bags, no pens, no dignity, and no choice. Once across the bridge, the erosion of your conscious choice begins. There is the surrendering of the one thing that displays your identity, your id—driver's license, identification card, or passport. You are then issued a generic faceless prison pass. Then comes the hand stamp of invisible black- light ink that we not so affectionately called "radioactive tracing dye." This invisible stamp is the only thing that gives the semblance of being a person instead of a "package" (as inmates are often called.)

After passing through numerous metal detectors and being constantly reminded by your very own correction officer not to lose your prison id or they will keep you there, you are at your destination. For us, that was the Island Academy on the Juvenile Detention Center. Here we trade in one Riker's pass for another more specific to the area. More metal detectors. More orders yelled at you. More red tape. More stripping of your humanness.

Finally, there it is, the mess hall where we are to meet a group of adolescent boys who are numerically on the brink of manhood, but mentally experienced men. A large white tent-shaped structure looms before us. As we enter—SMACK!—The smell hits you. Stale urine, disinfectant, remnants of the K-9 unit. This is where they eat. Say it with me. THIS IS WHERE THEY EAT. We separate into classrooms and begin to get to know each other.

Constant Interruptions. Correction Officers. Loud Demands. Constant reminders of who is boss. Then a student/inmate is called out only to return with physical evidence of manhandling. Around his neck and his eyes there lie red handprints displaying the chokehold he received only a few minutes before. It hurts. It hurts his pride. It hurts my heart. Nothing can be done!?!

We went to Rikers with the intent of sharing information with the students. We wanted to discuss the nature of the Prison Industrial Complex, past movements and struggles, art, and their views of their experiences at Rikers. What we got was distinctly more important. They talked, we listened, and whenever possible they wrote things down. While we were trying desperately to get the students of Rikers Island Academy to produce a physical product, they were trying desperately to educate us. It was not what they wrote or drew, it was what they taught us that was important to them.

To never have a moment's peace. To never be able to be alone with your thoughts, let alone have a complete one. I cannot fathom not being able to think, yet that is the reality of prison. The students described what it is like to be incessantly interrupted. Every time you begin to wrap your brain around an idea, they—the correction officers—are there to wield the power of the system. Nothing can be done!?!

Ironically, we went with the idea that they would be interested in what we were interested in—liberation. We talked about the movement in South Africa to end apartheid. We talked about the Black Panther Party, the Black Power Movements. We talked movements. Resistance. They talked punishments. Powerlessness. Deserving. They showed us their world. A world where they believed that their crimes made them responsible for their condition. A condition that made them feel defenseless, and unable to facilitate change.

The conditions. They told us of their conditions. They described how the only choices that they were able to make involved buying things for the commissary. They talked of harsh soaps and toothpastes that were only suitable for washing clothes. They described how using the soap on their skin was a disaster waiting to happen. The result, no skin. They talked of bad skin, bad food and no sleep. Segregated quarters for gays. Drugs. Cigarettes. Fights. Survival. They talked about how to survive.

The hardest thing for them to talk about was the people they were hurting because they are in jail. Mothers. Girlfriends. Visitors. Love. To get them to talk about what they felt, thought and remembered about a woman they left at home, I told them about the man I left at home. I opened up and relived my ex's five year stint in California. They wondered if I remained faithful, if their loves will remain faithful. They acknowledged the pain that incarceration causes.

Stereotypes. Statistics. Cause and effect. We hoped that they would see the complexity of the Prison Industrial Complex. Somehow, we wanted to convince them that it was not their fault they were in prison. Or were we? It is strange to talk of how society, the system, the man are responsible for their incarceration, while in the next conversation we are preaching to them to change their lifestyle. If the true belief is that they are not responsible/ at fault then it is society, the system, the matrix that should change, not them. Yet still, we talked about future changes to lead to possibility.

Most of them talked of not returning to prison. They talked about going home, changing their ways, and moving to a new phase in life. It was hard to believe. The hope that they would really change was there, but the doubt was there also, occupying the same space. Who knows where it came from. Maybe it was cynicism. Maybe it was seeing so many others making the same promises to change, and always falling back into their own ways. Maybe it is because the system does not allow it. Only a few are able to escape.

To understand the Prison Industrial Complex is to understand that it does not want to let go of any human being. It feeds on poverty. It feeds on racism. It feeds on capitalism. It makes one of the most natural desires to escape life's woes a crime. Then incarcerates the "criminal." Once caged, it strips you of your ability to make a living, vote for better conditions, or move away from the conditions that caused your "criminal" behavior in the first place. It has you! No money. The same environment. The same lonely road back into the belly of the beast.

When we talked about a way out, or a new way it was hard to grasp. To envision a world without prisons was difficult to say the least. To envision a new system, uncorrupted and free, was impossible. To believe that they had a chance of changing their situation was incomprehensible. A world without a Prison Industrial Complex…

You need to be on your shit to control
it brings order to the way you like it
the way you should be

Power earns respect

But why do I need respect

IT MEANS NOTHING AND EVERYTHING TO ME

In jail, you have the leaders and the team
In the country you have the president

If you don't fight you don't have respect

And if you don't respect us, you owe money

You owe money **means**

You earned an ass kicking

Bow wow
10/8/07

win you r in jell you have to B on your shit uf you not you well get fucked up

Ain't nothing better than freedom. As long as I'm out in the world, and I'm not on probation.

Probation is a set-up. We have to eat food they give us.

In the world, you don't have to wear state clothes. We don't have a washing machine.

Slaves. Got to get up when they tell us.

You don't have to watch your back all the time,

in here you do. You need to protect yourself-- that's why people die in jail.

This right here is a lesson about the things in life. You can't trust nobody

in jail. If you have somebody,

and grow up, there's nothing he can do for you that you can't do

for yourself. Now I know what I got to do.

HE SAID
HE OWNED HER
BODY AND SOUL

he had her cooking and cleaning
9 months pregnant
still working
BACK ACHING cause she been scrounging for nickels and dimes

her man ain't worth shit
but she still with him cause she opened her legs
and he got her pregnant
and she don't want to raise her child on her own
there are already too many fatherless sons out there
so she would rather a deadbeat dad
that's around instead of one that's nonexistent
she don't ask him to get a job
cause when she did before he got vicious
slammed an iron in her head
she had to get 24 stitches
almost killed her so she shut her mouth
and let her soul die
allowed herself to shrivel up inside

he said he owned her
body and soul

and he did
cause she had relinquished her power to him

I think that we can't change the system because it's their job, people get paid to put us behind bars. Also, if we all were to come together and try to fight the system it wouldn't do much. It would only change a little, not much. I don't even think that the judge cares about you. It's his or her job to sentence you.

They don't care if your family is crying or how decent you dress for court. If they don't like you or if the judge woke up in a bad mood, they are the ones with the power. I think that our words don't mean anything to the judge because if they did I wouldn't need a lawyer, I would defend myself because I know what I did, and all I do is tell my lawyer and he goes and tells the same thing. I really don't think we can change the system.

So now I can finally find Rikers on a subway map. Wanna learn? Locate LaGuardia airport, look about an inch to the left and you will see a white box barely outlining the shape that it's covering.

That's Rikers.

Hidden from view. Outta sight, outta mind. No one wants to think about a jail, especially no one on a subway coming from a long day at the office, or a guy trying to spend some time with his girlfriend, or someone visiting the city for the first time, or someone taking their freedom for granted hopping a flight from New York to Paris, or Africa, or Los Angeles. Cover it, because if we don't see it, then we don't have to think about it. And if we don't have to think about it, then it really doesn't even exist. This is how we think.

I think in some situations you don't have to do anything and it would fall into place. And on the other hand, demonstration is essential so one can get results for the better and be willing to take a stand for what one believes in. Because we all know some things we have control of and some things we don't.

Youth Voices on Lockdown
An Anthology of Creative Writing

By students at the Sprungs section of
Island Academy – Rikers Island

Edited with commentary by students in Columbia
University's course, "Youth Voices on Lockdown"

Spring 2004

Power is respect that you contain

Power is the threat that you maintain

Power is being above even if you are not a thug

Power is instead of shooting them slugs

    you pay someone to do it for you

Power is money and respect

Power is fear if they fear you, you are fearful

Power is love if you show love you get love

Power is standing tall no matter what, something like a tower

I thought I had it all planned
In my journey through life
Hustling on the street corners n breaking night
Making fast money but what was it all worth
Addicted to the streets I think I've been cursed
Dreams of getting rich and going legit
But all I seen in my future is this jail shit
I'm lost I'm trying to find my path
Every time I get close I'm lured by a demon called cash
How long will this battle of good n evil in me last? I don't know
But what I do know is I have to make this choice past
cause time seems like it's going
in a flash I need to realize
that life in the streets isn't all I have.

justice
illustrious
ridiculous
manipulous
tug of war
freedom no more
held under water
washed up on shore
dragged by my feet
no promises to keep
skinned knees, nothing to bleed
protection?
how bout repression
perplexion
anti-affection
complete rejection
a c-section
pull out my soul
and then you'll patrol
keep me underground
not to make a sound
rip out my voice
you think I'm your toy
now I'm all wound up
about to erupt
enslaved
it's corruption.
i need a revolution.
clear out your pollution.
destroy institution.
equal substitution.
loves infusion.
my hearts resolution.

We're all criminals really
How many laws have you broken in the last week?
How many times in your life
have you done something
you aren't supposed to do
when no one was looking?
And how many times
was somebody looking?

Luck.

How many times have you been judged
because of your age, your race, the clothes you wear?
We're all people.
Rules are meant to be broken
and we seem to
have a nasty habit of
mistrusting one another.

Wrong place, wrong time
shit out of luck.

So I'm sitting with this kid
and he's talking all this stuff
about this story we just read.
Tell the truth, ain't just fluff.
But his right to education
in this fucked up racist nation

                              means his mind just goes to waste,
                              means his mind just goes to waste.

See the thing they say he needs
is to be able to read,
because they say he can't just think,
and they say he can't just be.

But what do they do for a kid who came this far?
And how can he make it if they're raising the bar?
But they're leaving him behind—

his mind, his mind.

                              Means his mind just goes to waste,
                              means his mind just goes to waste.

When wrong has been committed, the perpetrator and perpetrated must reconcile themselves to an agreed solution, to a way forward. Equal participants in a discussion should approach each other in openness.

Our obligations to each other draw from our mutual vulnerabilities.

Paralysis- which wrongs require a right? Who decides when I have transgressed? At what point do we give up and accept fate?

Justice is a little bit of playing god: of deciding when to accept change and when to demand the world stay the same.

Justice is the play of fate between two or more hands, deciding a way to the future that merges left, right, and wrong in the suffering confusion of human existence.

Fight for what you believe in and find the truth about things that don't make sense to you. One of the correction officers told me a saying "If you fight to make a point and you know that you are right, take it as far as you could take whatever it is, even if you die for what you believe in to make a point."

Another thing that a correction officer told me, a saying "Menace 2 Society," that means that the government comes first in doing things, then the Jail System comes second. Like the book I read, Behold a Pale Horse by William Cooper, it is about a CIA agent giving cut information because people should know what is going on. He was fighting for what he believes in and the Big brothers killed him. The big brothers is the government.

Lesson inspired by the Black Panther's Ten Point Program on social, economic and political rights.

TEN POINT PLAN:

1. I want freedom so that I can finish school.
2. I want my freedom so that I can get my life together.
3. I want my freedom so that I can be with my family.
4. I want my freedom so that I can make a family.
5. I want my freedom so that I can be successful
6. I want the freedom to make mistakes.
7. I want a proper education.
8. I want to know my rights.
9. I want my life back.
10. I want freedom.

Being here is not fair because of the way some people want to control everything, they don't want the little people to get on the phone they take their food they just rob them, and that's not fair for the little guy or for the people who can't stand up for themselves. If I could control some things in here I would make sure every body gets on the phone and be fair to all the little guys who can't stand up for themselves.

This place is very fucked up that's it basically!

The system is not fair, because I personally think that the system is built to enslave all ghetto youths and to keep pushing them down so they could never rise to the top.

The system knows that to keep poor people from rising is to slay us, imprison us, and even cheat us out of our rights.

We need to get together and fight the system because if we don't it's going to get to a point where we are not going to be able to stop it (the system).

REFLECTIONS ON THE SYSTEM:

The system is not fair, because I personally think that the system is built to enslave all ghetto youths and to keep pushing them down so they can never rise to the top.

The system knows that to keep poor people from rising you have to slay us,

imprison us, and even cheat us out of our rights.

We need to get together and fight the system because if we don't, it's going to get to a point where we are not going to be able to stop it (the system).

— Rafique

I think that we can't change the system because it's their job, people get paid to put us behind bars. Also if we all were to come together and try to fight the system it wouldn't do much. It would only change a little, not much. I don't even think that the judge cares about you. Its his or her job to sentence you.

They don't care if your family is crying or how decent you dress for court. If they don't like you or if the judge woke up in a bad mood, they are the ones with the power. I think that our words don't mean anything to the judge because if they did I wouldn't need a lawyer, I would defend myself because I know what I did, and all I do is tell my lawyer and he goes and tells the judge the same thing.
I really don't think we can change the system.

— Leon

You see a term like **freedom**
when you say liberty and justice for all
you know how in the bible you will be served justice

Justice for all.

A high-class word
that can be used in a lot of different terms
or it can be bogus.

The word is out there for no reason,
they say justice for all
but the government does not apply to all.
They just want certain people to apply to it.

Justice is just for us,

people that are non-rich.

They put it out there for us.

Thou shall not kill,
thou shall not steal
does not apply to the rich.

They only tell it to us
so we won't do it.

If I could get revenge on my

    friend who told,

Without his words not a soul would

    have known.

If it were true that would not be so

    bad,

Knowing that it is not makes me

    sad.

My revenge will not be for

    children to see,

His face all lumped up,

    blood on his white T.

Wrong choices are like wrong

    answers,

My heart says no but my body just

    answers.

Listen Judge I only got one life
to live. Bring me to jail
so I could not make any kids.
I only 17, tryin to make the green.
Cops wanna knock down,
lock me, keeping my life on fuckin floppy,
coping work from poppy, got me running down
lots B, I ain't trying get shout, see.
Putting me in a cell only make me cocky.

When I was in Rikers you was in diapers. I was in Syfers, rhyming with lifers. You was at home trying to get tighter.

When you was trying to get tighter them fucking police came and locked me up so the DA tried to indict me but fuck them niggas they just like us. I got a Jewish lawyer nigga so I got to beat the charges.

They thought they was going to take away my freedom but now I'm back home, talking on the phone. My money long so I ain't got to go to the courtroom no more. This shit is unreal, it's wrong. But guess what, I got the judge's bitch in a red see through thong.

The lesson from last week went over rather well. Amanda and I wrote out tasks and responsibility for the entire group so the transitions and entrances were smooth. The hip-hop machine went over better than I had expected. Well in actuality it went over just as well as I had expected, though there were others that shall remain nameless (Bryonn) that felt that the activity may not work. Luckily it did and we had fun while getting a feel for everyone's personality and self-expression. The highlight of the secession for me was the battle. Ronald and "Blue Hefner" battled each other and crushed it. I was excited to see Blu go because he did not perform the class before when Ronald went, so I was glad to see he accepted the healthy challenge. However I did have to make an executive decision to remodel the closing activity to omit the word swagger-jack from the assignment. It was clear after Ronald saying that he did not read other people lyrics because they reflect in his work, that the idea of using another person's style is exactly what they did not want to do. And I was fine with that as long as everyone felt like they are in a place where they feel safe to express their ideas and viewpoints.

I am still pondering on the comment made by Danae and the reactions from one of the students. Danae referred to the students as "Rikers students" in the beginning of class and got an interesting reaction. A student responded by saying "Wow Rikers students wow". Danae did not hear him, and neither did most people so nothing was said. I heard but I didn't say anything either, I guess I didn't want to throw off the momentum of the class. Just like I did not say anything about Ronald saying his favorite song by Jay-Z was "Big Pimpin" because Jay is pimping bitches and may have pimped me. My response was quick and sharp saying, or maybe he pimped you, or maybe your mother?" I then asked him how would he feel if someone did say something like that about his mother, as did Bryonn. Yet the issue was still brushed over, and it should have been addressed. I agree that moments like these should be addressed when they happen and taken care of at that moment. It does not benefit anyone to sweep these kinds of things under some imaginary rug. The power dynamics in the room seem to be closely related to the idea of the oppressed and the oppressor that Assata Shakur discusses. The young men often feel oppressed by the PIC, which closely relates to being oppressed by their external neighborhood environment. In addition they may feel oppressed by the treatment they will receive once they return from being incarcerated. Yet in that same respect they act as the oppressor in relation to women and the role they play in society. I feel that this dynamic is very interesting and should also be discussed in a future class.

When the *nock* on the door is unexpected
you never no what to expect,
after the nocks then come the

BANG.

If only imaginary and it
creates images of a place you
never thought you would see.

But it's not a dream when
you hear another unexpected

NOCK

**that's the judge slamming the gravel
to let you know he won't set you free.**

Now everything becomes unexpected
until the day your set free.

I be thinking about how my lifestyle has affected my everyday life now. All cause of my hunger and need to cover up myself in certain kinds of clothes. As well as wanting to be looked at a certain way by my peers. So when my guardians couldn't do it for me or refused to do so, I took it upon myself. But I had no job, just my mind and my courage to sell drugs and rob every time I felt as if I was slacking.

But now *I'm locked up for that same hunger* so I can say that my life will be different when I leave here because I will appreciate the little things that I constantly took for granted.

I say my hunger and my need to dress a certain kind of way because of how some of our younger brothers and sisters mind is caught up in the fashion world and how to deal with it. Not really acceptance but a certain kind of respect on reaction to your presence. (Real pity I say this because its true, for example if you try to talk to a young lady in my generation 1 out of 10 she is going to look at your physical appearance and that's sad cause you could be a nice person. So this behavior has an effect on me as well as a lot of other younger people. And it makes me feel as if I have to dress nice.)

I would get revenge
on the judge
who sent me here
he didn't even
give me a chance

He just read my case
and put me away

He really didn't
even let me say
anything to redeem
myself

So in my eyes,
he really didn't care

But it doesn't matter,
I'M HERE NOW...

I could have
told the judge
what really happened
but he probably
wouldn't care

He would have
still sent me HERE

LOVE is my mother and my family, my hood, and my everything that means something to me.

HATE is the white man justice (aka-court-aka-judge) and where I am at now.

Also, HATE is seeing and having my mother cry every night and my bad habits that I have now and in the past.

I HATE myself for putting myself in this predicament and crying myself to sleep every night.

The man I am type of lazy

The man I am don't let words faze me

The man I am is not scared

The man I am do not fear

The man I am wish I can fly

The man I am will not lie

The man I am is in jail

The man I am is going thru Hell

The man I am love manhood

The man I am love the hood

The man I am Hope is near

The man I am Hope is scarce

Release Date: 3-8-07

I'm 18 years old from the Castle Hill Projects in the Bronx. I have a great mom, brothers Timothy and Christopher, and my sister Tiffany.

My goals are to be somebody and finish school. I also want to be your favorite rapper or basketball player, because I'm good at both. I leave Rikers on March 8, 2007.

Release Date: 4-7-07

I'm 18 years old from Flatbush, Brooklyn. I have five brothers, 2 sisters, and one on the way.

My accomplishments and ambitions include trying to get my GED, go home, and not come back to jail.

When I go home, I want to go to college and to get a degree in business, and start a family of my own and live to tell my kids what I have been through in my life.

Release Date: 12-29-06

I'm a 17 year old African American/West Indian/Dominican, born and raised in Harlem. I have one brother, and one sister.

My accomplishments include getting a GED, and having a baby boy any day now! One aspiration I have is to become an electrician.

My release date from the belly of the beast is December 29, 2006. As I write this, I have 14 days left.

Shout out to uptown, downtown, Westside, and eastside.
Harlem world one!

Release Date 1-28-07

I'm 18 years old, and of Black and Spanish decent. I was born and raised in the Bronx, NY.

I obtained my GED and will be going to college in the Spring of 2007 to work towards a degree in the medical field.

I would like to give a shout out to the Black government!!

Release Date: 3-19-07

I just turned 18 on December 1st, and I never thought I would make it. I'm from Far Rockaway, Queens Edgemere Projects. I'm Jamaican, and come from a fairly large family. I have an older brother and sister, and a nephew.

I would like to accomplish getting my GED, becoming a better person, and most of all going home. I would also like to become a successful Black person.

I wanna give a shout out to all of my fans and anybody who believes in me. Also, to all my Queens people.

Release Date: 3-4-07

I am seventeen years old. I grew up in a foster home with three sisters. Around the age of nine, I was adopted and only one of my sisters was able to come with me. Unfortunately, I have not seen my other two sisters in about eight years. As for my current family, I have my adoptive mother, my sisters, and my unborn child on the way.

My life's accomplishments so far have been overcoming certain negativities. Also, I have grasped the concept of better learning and why it is fundamental to go to school. I have bettered myself physically, mentally, and educationally.

My aspirations in life are to become a nurse so I can help sick people. I would like to be a registered nurse, and would like to get my master's degree someday. Also, I would like to become a motivational speaker to help troubled youth. My release date is March 4, 2007.

For every bodys dedication I'd like to show appreciation for every thing taught and every skill baught from raps to poems and every body joined I feel out of everything I been In this is the nicest For feelings and programs skills it was priceless.

now this class is good it helps me get past my past and just laugh at the shit I past now I used to do poetry this class got me back in toch with my human being got me ahotic me and who am post to be see I was tacking me lightly not seeing me to my best abilyte like taking heid to thing I been notising I got a gift in the power to proform put my all in it and people ~~appreshit~~ adoor it I got people that see more in me than I can see and I'm blaiming people for the things that I'm doing c so I'm saying people got control of me Hell no only me can have control of me my mind open like the ocean c cause now who am sopost to be that being what I want to be by enay means nesasare cause thing aint hard they just compleeated not meaning I canit do it but I g just got to put my all in to it stop loseing and start gaining useing my brain to get my way in at the of this class there only one thing I'm ~~chose~~ ant thats me

When it was time to go, I almost didn't want to leave.

I started organizing and packing stuff to go. I was surprised that people were coming up to me and saying goodbye. People I hadn't even exchanged words with came to say bye. When I was leaving Jean said to me in Haitian Creole, *I'll be home soon.* I was touched. When we were waiting for the bus, I stayed by myself for a while and I let tears fall out my eyes. It was intense. On the train ride home, I wrote a rant/poem that was more about my state of mind than the experience itself...it is an accurate account on how I am changing (as a human being) because of this experience.

Hip hop means...

Hip hop is a means of expression, for people who don't have anything in there life positive to express themselves, hip-hop is there, like a friend, father or mentor. It seems extreme but people including me live for this. The thrill of whether people like your stuff or not. When you writing a rhyme or anything you let things go or you write things in your music that you don't even remember thinking. Because hip-hop brings a side out of you, that you don't see in everyday life, hip-hop is a medicine, it helps those whose life is dipped in sin helps them get through these problems by themselves.

Hip-hop is mysterious like a disease with no cure. Once you start you cant stop. Hip-hop. The blood that runs through the veins of human beings is as consistent, everlasting and unstoppable as hip-hop. Hip-hop means the start of a new life. The problem solver. It gives you a chance to redeem yourself, maybe not to others but definitely to yourself. In all, hip-hop cant be defined. The most direct or solid definition of hip-hop would be "a chance, a change, and a little strange" the words of the famous legend Rev Run.

Revolutionary Pedagogy

Introduction

by Ella Turenne

When it came time to listen to "A Change is Gonna Come" by Sam Cooke and write about "struggle" and "hope," all of the students were very eager to share their work to a beat or acappella. The rhymes the students came up with on the dot were deep. They were real. The students were very encouraging of each other and urged NYU students to share their own work. I think all in all, we were best connected and focused this time. I think the ground rules of respect, one mic, and self-determination sunk in.

—Kayleigh, NYU Student

Revolution. Say that word too loudly in Rikers and you raise suspicion, perhaps even alarm. ***Lyrics on Lockdown*** is a class that uses revolutionary pedagogy to raise consciousness and foster change. Change in thoughts. Change in actions. Change in state of mind, state of being. College students and Rikers students – some from different walks of life, some from the same walks of life – come together to create a liberated space within one that is meant to confine. We use this dichotomy to examine how art can be used as a tool for positive social change. For two to three hours each week, we are all free of the things that incarcerate us the most - jail, laws, work, school, authority, preconceptions.

A recent article in the New York Times claims that black men are in a state of emergency.[1] Studies conducted by Ivy League institutions, far removed from the ugly realities of the prison system, found that "Especially in the country's inner cities... finishing high school is the exception, legal work is scarcer than ever and prison is almost routine, with incarceration rates climbing for blacks even as urban crime rates have declined."[2] New York Times reporter Brent Staples stated at a recent New School for Social Research conference on punishment in America that there is a culture in urban communities that expects young black men will go to prison.

Studies have shown that the arts and education offer effective ways - financially and programmatically - of tackling the prison crisis.³ Year after year, politicians continue to ignore the call from grassroots organizers and communities to deal with the underlying causes of incarceration. Poverty. Poor education. A corporatized health care system. And of course, racism. The fear that they will appear soft on crime is great, so draconian policies such as the Rockefeller Drug Laws stay on the books.

The recent reforms occurring in school systems nationwide have not enhanced education. Instead, students are less prepared to become critical thinkers and are forced to learn in criminalized environments. In New York City, the Department of Education designated the most "problematic" schools as "Impact Schools," inundating them with police. The result? A clear school-to-prison pipeline. A strong signal to urban youth that they are expected to amount to nothing but a number at Rikers. Instead of examining why it costs over $200,000 a year to keep one youth in a New York City detention center but costs barely over $11,000 to keep that same youth in public school for a year, New York City (and many other cities in the US) chooses to continue perpetuating the systematic oppression of young people.

One might think a class can't change all that. However, in each of the students in a Lyrics on Lockdown class, there is the potential for change. In the class, among college and incarcerated students are future lawyers, policy makers, artists and community organizers. These are the leaders of tomorrow whose perception of the prison industrial complex is shaped by their experiences together. bell hooks said "The classroom remains the most radical space for possibility in the academy.⁴" That's why it's revolutionary.

Agó? Amé!

That's how we respectfully get each other's attention in a *Lyrics on Lockdown class*. It is the Swahili term for "Are you listening? You've got my attention." Lyrics on Lockdown translation: **One Mic**.

This is critical because in a *Lyrics on Lockdown* class, everyone owns the pedagogy. It is a pedagogy rooted in critical analysis, Friere's pedagogy of the oppressed and Boal's theatre of the oppressed. We emphasize the fact that everyone has something to bring to the table and no one person's experience trumps anyone else's. In this classroom we are all artists examining power and oppression, working together towards transformation of ourselves and our communities. Our tools: pens, paper, music, lyrics, chalk, blackboards, crayons, paint, our bodies and minds.

For the college student taking this class, it is an intense experience. The first seven weeks are spent reading and discussing the intricacies of the prison industrial complex, radical social movements, arts and social change, hip-hop and spoken word and race and class in America. It is a lot to cover in seven weeks, but necessary to build a solid framework with which to understand and think critically about the prison industrial complex. The students are then asked to create arts based workshops which they facilitate with students at Island Academy, one of the high schools at Riker's Island. The emphasis is on facilitating, not teaching. We all recognize that everyone in the classroom is facilitating and learning simultaneously. *Agó? Amé!*

> "The raison d'être of liberation education lies in its drive towards reconciliation. Education must begin with the solution of the teacher-student contradiction, by reconciling the poles of the contradiction so that both are simultaneously teachers and students."
> —Paolo Friere[5]

Freire's idea is one that is naturally challenged by mainstream canons of education theory. This model, however, has been critical to the success of Lyrics on Lockdown. Quite literally, this space of creation, as put by one of the Rikers students, is one of the few times while incarcerated when students feel free. That piece of freedom, no matter how small, becomes extremely important.

Each workshop is centered on a social justice related theme and includes ice breakers, presentations and discussions in the first half of the session. The second half is usually devoted to free writes, group poem development, or other group art pieces and activities. The work you have read in this anthology is a result of individual and group work created from these student developed workshops. Vital elements of each lesson include critical thinking, fostering literacy and working through various complex social, historical and contemporary issues. This model works because we use a language common to all of us: art, hip hop and spoken word.

> *Remember that there is only one important time and that is now. The present moment is the only time over which we have domination. The most important person is always that person you are with, who is right before you, for who knows if you will have dealings with any other person in the future? The most important pursuit is making the person standing at your side happy, for that alone is the pursuit of life.*
>
> —Thich Nhat Hanh[6]

I became involved with **Lyrics on Lockdown** on my first national tour in 2002. It was an amazing experience, performing and organizing. I was fresh out of social work school, looking to put into practice all the community organizing theories I had learned from two of my esteemed faculty mentors, Lee Stapes and Melvin Delgado. As an artist, I needed to do that through the arts. Blackout seemed to be the only organization dedicated to organizing around the arts by people of color, for people of color.

Those early years of **Lyrics on Lockdown** were rough and emotionally draining. We had little funding, literally selling posters during performances to finance our next meal. The scope of what had to be done to transform the prison industrial complex loomed over us like pregnant cloud before a storm. It was all around us, in our families and communities. We were personally affected by prisons. Yet we kept doing it. We didn't ask ourselves why because the answer was simple really. The prison crisis was a matter of life and death.

Since then, ***Lyrics on Lockdown*** has morphed into a national movement. Hundreds of college and incarcerated youth have come together, in spite of differences in race, socioeconomic status and education level, to create art with themes of social justice. The lesson plans that follow are included in the hopes that they will build awareness, foster dialogue and inspire more creative work from youth.

Lyrics on Lockdown's mission has always been to educate people about the prison crisis. Along with that we have sought to inspire change and open space for voices on lockdown to speak and be heard. This anthology represents youth voices on lockdown who have spoken loudly, with passion and presence. As the prolific Sekou Sundiata put it – America is in the classroom.

---

1 Erik Eckholm, "Plight Deepens for Black Men, Studies Warn," New York Times, March 20, 2006.

2 Ibid

3 Community Arts Network, A Journey of Discouragement and Hope: An Introduction to Arts and Corrections, http://www.communityarts.net/readingroom/archivefiles/2001/12/a_journey_of_di.php (December, 2001).

4 hooks, b. Teaching to Transgress. Routledge (1994)
5 Freire, P. Pedagogy of the Oppressed. Continuum International Publishing Group (1993).

6 Hanh, T. N. The Miracle of Mindfulness. Beacon Press. (1999)

Ice Breakers

Everyone stands in a circle, shoulder to shoulder, facing each other. One person starts in the center of the circle and yells out a quality about him or herself (ie. I have a sister, I have lived abroad, I hate mushrooms, my favorite rapper is Jay-Z, etc.) Whoever else has this quality runs into the center of the circle and has to return to an empty spot in the circle made by the other people running into the center (this is why it is important to stand shoulder to shoulder so that the open spots are obvious, there is purposely one less spot than bodies since one person began in the center.) It is like musical chairs but standing up. The last person left in the circle who does not have a spot to stand is now the person that calls out the quality.

Divide into small groups of around four or five. Each group is given a word - e.g. "Time". Each person writes down or remembers two or three words or phrases associated with the theme, e.g. *slow, fast, boredom, quickly, centuries*. Now the group has to make an object out of the members, linked to the theme (such as a clock). Ideally the object should move. Next the group brings the object to life and works out a way of bringing in some or all of their words - linked to their movements. They show the resulting *People Poem* to the rest of the class, who can try and guess the theme. Themes could include: colors, emotions, elements - *earth, air, fire, water,* opposites - *cold/hot, fast/slow, high/low*.

Students break into groups of 3 or 4 partners. Facilitator gives one word such as "brother." Teams take alternate turns singing a line from songs that contain that word (encourage silliness). First team to sing a song with that word wins.

Rhyme Circle - break into groups, each group will sit in a circle and take turns rhyming words, going around clockwise, and then gradually working into short phrases, and sentences.

Everyone will come up with a short rhyme that includes their name. Another option is the Name Pantomime icebreaker, where everyone comes up with a verb that is the same letter as their name, and does an action to go along with it (i.e. Jumping James). Then everyone repeats the name and does the action.

Everyone stands up in a large circle and one by one, going around the circle each person enters the center of the group. Students from Island Academy explain their tag name to the group, and visitors explain their own nicknames so that everyone is following the same pattern.

Wagon Wheel – Select a group to form the inner circle and provide each individual with a different question. Have the remaining people form the outer circle. The inside circle asks their partner in the outside circle their question, and then the outside partner asks the inside person the same question--each person has 30 seconds to speak. Inner circle moves to the right for each new question, so that by the end of the activity everyone has asked and answered each question in a personal setting. Introduce yourself by name and school with each new person.

The Machine – a theme will be given (power, love, greed, hate) and each person in the group must come into the center of the circle and create a sound and motion that goes with that theme. Each person on the outside of the circle must add to that until everyone comes into the circle, creating a machine.

*It is very important to practice icebreakers to make sure that you understand them fully, and can facilitate them effectively. When done well, they set the perfect tone for collaboration.

POWER & PROPAGANDA

"How do these concepts emerge in hip hop and spoken word?"

OBJECTIVES:
Using the words and images of Tupac, Noam Chomsky, and Assata Shakur, students will explore the concepts of power and propaganda; and how those ideologies affect and inform their lives, how they communicate, how society/others view them, and their affects/influence on the prison industrial complex.

MATERIALS:
CD player, DVD player, TV, copies of poem/lyrics/text, pens, blank paper, folders

ICE BREAKER:
Introductions (20 min): Two Truths & One Lie
Everyone will stand in a circle. Each person will enter the center of the circle and say two things that are true about themselves, and one lie. The group has to guess which is the lie.

WORKSHOP CORE:
Introduce topic. Define terms: propaganda, power, hip- hip, and spoken word. (10 min)

TUPAC RESURECTION- (15 min)
*(the clip is on 'Thug Life', and the media's distortion of the meaning.) Discussion: Where was the propaganda? What was the message they were trying to purport? Who has the power here? What is the power dynamic?

NOAM CHOMSKY- (15 min)
*Hand out and read piece "Public Relations" from *Media Control (pg 24, 26)*. *Discuss Chomsky piece, his definition of propaganda, and its relation or connection to the Tupac video clip, and hip hop in general.

LABELING- Are you truly the label you wear?
(small groups/ 20-30 min)

Revolutionary Pedagogy 133

*Place labels on foreheads of all participants, put them in small groups, have them talk to each other as if the person is that label. Can't reveal or guess the label, etc. Everyone must be treated like his/her label. After 10 min, come back together and discuss how it felt being treated based on the label. Did they begin to act like the label? In relation to the Tupac piece, how was he treated based on the labels placed on him? How do labels affect policy and prisons? Have you been labeled? As what? How were you treated? Touch on power. Who has the power in labeling? Is that a form of propaganda?

ASSATA ON EDUCATION- Is it propaganda? Who has the power? (10 min)
*Handout reading, an excerpt from *Assata: An Autobiography,* by Assata Shakur.
*Discuss her statement on education. How have we been "educated" in relation to power and propaganda? Regarding her statement on the need for education outside of the school system, what should or shouldn't we learn?

FREEWRITE: Prompt: "Power is..."(10 min)

WRAP UP: Share work and discuss it. Recap themes of lesson/ discussion. (15 min)

CRIMINAL BEHAVIOR
"I didn't have a record till I had a record" -Tupac

OBJECTIVES:
Students will have a strong sense of the power of rhetoric and language in codifying power structures and relations. The language of dehumanization, is the same language of slavery, which justifies imprisonment. Questions the lesson plan will cover: What is crime and who defines it? Who has the power to define this term? Are people criminal? Can societies, institutions, or police be considered criminal? Is what goes on inside prison walls-the cruel and unusual punishment, violation of human rights, or free slave labor? Are these things more criminal that the acts done by socially-defined "criminals?"

MATERIALS:
TV, DVD player, CD player, paper, pencils, copies of readings

ICE BREAKER: Zip, zap, zoom (5 min)

WORKSHOP CORE:
Film Clip: "HIGHER LEARNING" (15 min)
*View scene: Omar Epps wrongly accused of a crime. Discuss alternative explanations

THEATRE of the OPPRESSED (Alternative Newspaper Readings Game (75 min))
*Break up into groups, assign each group a case. Students volunteer to construct an alternative scenario to the one reported in the article. (Reading/Skits- 30 min)
*Present skits in class (5-10 min)
    *Discuss what they might have done differently. (5-10) min
    *Re-group, apply suggestions from discussion in reenactment. (5-10 min)
*Discussion on institutional and social crime. What can society do to prevent that crime? Are societies and or institutions criminal for producing, encouraging, and not preventing crime? Is there a cultural

legacy and historical celebration on crime in America? How is the theft of people and land different than the theft for which "criminals" today are imprisoned? (10-15 min)

TUPAC (15 min)
>   *play "Words of Wisdom." How does Tupac define "criminal"?
>   *play "America's Nightmare." Who is America's worst nightmare?

PARIS (10 min)
>   *play "Evil" by Paris. How does Paris define what is criminal? What is evil?

"PERUVIAN COCAINE" Middle Class verse (5 min)
*How is middle class criminality viewed differently from the conventional criminal?

FREE WRITE: Prompt: Connect the terms THUG LIFE and CRIMINAL. (20 min)
*Create a poem using the letters in the word CRIMINAL.

WRAP UP: Share work in open mic. (15 min)

STEPPING OUT OF YOUR COMFORT ZONE
Physical Movement in Relation to Social Movements

OBJECTIVES:
Answer the question "How does the body relate to social activism?" by exploring the tension between movements that are comfortable versus strange or foreign.

MATERIALS:
TV, DVD player, space to choreograph movements

ICEBREAKER: (20min)
This is a variation on a game called Stupid Ninja Game. We will each be choosing a movement and a way of saying our name. We will go around the circle introducing our name and movement, the rest of the group imitating each person's movement and repeating their name in the same fashion. After we have completed this introduction, we will go around one more time to familiarize ourselves with each other's sound/movement. In the game, a person is to do their sound/movement and then another person's. That person then receives it and passes it on to another person by doing their own sound/movement and another person's. We will have a practice round, and then we will play with elimination. People will be eliminated for an extended pause or trying to pass it along to someone who is no longer in the circle.

WORKSHOP CORE

DISCUSSION: (10 min)
*Why were certain movements amusing? Does it matter who does the movement to make it seem normal or acceptable? Did you notice anyone purposely staying in or stepping out of his/her comfort zone?

VIDEO EXCERPTS (10min)
*Hand out a worksheet that lists 8 styles of dance along with a short description. Watch the video that shows 30 second clips of each style of dance. Each student take 30 seconds to read the dance description and check the box that says if reader would feel the movement is "me," "maybe

me," or "not me."

*Discussion: (10 min)

Who would feel comfortable doing: Krumping, Dunham, Capoeira, Ballet, Breakdance(1), Waltz, Breakdance (2), Quickstep, Rumba

GROUP ACTIVITY (20 min)

*Break everyone into small groups of 4-5 people.

*Each person choose something they are struggling with or have struggled with in their lives and create a short movement or two to represent it.

*Each group will then put the movements in a sequence that fits together, with everyone in the group doing the movements.

*The idea is to create a dance/movement sequence that is your group's own representation of struggle.

WRAP UP: (25 min)

The sequences will be performed for the entire class with or without music if space permits. Leave time for free styling in the circle.

HIP HOP AS THE VOICE OF BLACK & LATINO YOUTH FROM URBAN AREAS

"...the essence of hip hop is street poetry"

OBJECTIVES:
To understand how the whitewashing of history is subverted through hip hop and how you can use hip hop to tell your own story. To use the film "Hip Hop Immortals" to connect the history of hip hop, as a youth movement that came out of poor and working class Black and Latino communities in the South Bronx, to the historical invisibility of class stratification. To use discussion and writing activities to address these issues of invisibility from the perspective of the personal narrative.

MATERIALS:
TV, DVD, CD player or ipod w/ speakers, name tags, paper, pens, markers, post-it pad.

ICE BREAKER: (10 min)
The Machine (check ice breaker resource sheet): Hip Hop Theme

WORKSHOP CORE:
WATCH: (5 min) Film Clip "Hip Hop Immortals", pass put packet. Spoken word performance by facilitator (5min)

FREEWRITE: Prompt: "To me hip hop means..." (10 min)
Ask 3 volunteers to read their pieces & ask for a volunteer to write down reoccurring words/themes on easel pad (10 min)

DISCUSSION (10 min)
Do you feel like hip hop accurately portrays your environment? Do you feel like hip hop gives you a voice or a way to express yourself? Do you think hip hop has changed since you were younger? If so, in what way? Is it better, worse, or just different?

LYRICS (15-20 min)

Listen to Common Sense "I Used to Love H.E.R." close reading and discussion of lyrics. Listen to a song by Jay-Z "Party Life", close reading and discussion of lyrics. Compare and contrast the messages, devices and styles – how are they alike and how are they different? What do you like or what don't you like about each.

WRITING EXERCISE: (10 min)
Students will break into 4 groups and then be given a packet containing bios & lyrics of 5 different MCs. They will choose an MC to swagger jack their style in order to create a cohesive group piece that contains information about each individual student. Each student needs to include at least two lines about their own individual experience.

WRAP UP: At the end, we will have 2 rounds of battling. 2 groups at a time will use their pieces to battle. (10 min) The rest of the class will determine the winner by show of applause. (5 min)

Responsibility vs. Irresponsibility

OBJECTIVES:
Explore lyrical content and discuss the artist's responsibility.

MATERIALS:
Lyrics: Eminem "When the Music Stops", Lyrics: K'Naan "The African Way", Lyrics: Lupe Fiasco "Dumb It Down", Quotes Sheet, CD player

ICE BREAKER: (5 min)
Lyric Game (facilitators do example). One person starts out with a lyric from a song. The person repeats their lyric until another person jumps in with a different lyric. The lyric has to have a similar word or theme from the lyric before it.

WORKSHOP CORE:
DISCUSSION: Ask everybody what they thought about the lyric game? Which lyrics stood out to them? Think about how mainstream music becomes your reality and your instinct. What is responsibility? Free association? Share Webster definition of *Responsible*: "Able to respond or answer for one's conduct and obligations". Is an artist obligated to be responsible to their audience? (10 min)

EMINEM: Play song "When the Music Stops" (2 min)
Discussion: Close reading of Bizzare's last verse on taking lyrics too literally, discuss persona (D12 example) If every rapper has a persona can they really "keep it real"? Is the artist being imitated or the persona? Is Eminem talking about the problem enough? When are you articulating an issue and when are you endorsing it? (10 min)

K'NAAN: "The African Way" Play first half of song (2 min)
Discussion: What stood out? Focus on the global aspect; we talked about hip hop as a global culture. Does more power mean more responsibility? K'Naan says he is "taking it back" is it the choice of the artist to be responsible? Or is it more the listeners' responsibility to demand something with a message? (10 min)

FREEWRITE: Prompt: What does it mean to be an artist? (10 min)

LUPE FIASCO: Play song "Dumb It Down" (2 min)
Discussion: How can an artist be responsible be responsible when they are faced with outside pressures. Focus on other voices in the song. (Talk about him actively choosing to not bow to outside pressures.) We talked about hip hop as a reflection of society. Is there a standard of success? What is it? Does this limit the way success can be defined? (10 min)

GROUP ACTIVITY: Break up into groups. (15 min)
You are the artist. Choose a side in the debate about whether the artist has a responsibility to the audience?

WRAP UP: Open up the classroom debate, share opinions from groups. (10 min)

Radio Control

OBJECTIVES:
Examine radio as an artistic outlet to communicate, converse, provoke thought in others, and to convey ideas, concerns, questions, thoughts, viewpoints, and self expression. These may be in forms including, but not limited to, spoken word, lyricism, and poetry. Students create a piece of spoken word that conveys the truth of life in prison that is uncensored. Students feel as though they can freely express their feelings about family, life in prison, what life is going to be like when they are released. Develop an artistic outlet for their emotions that can be applied even after we leave.

MATERIALS:
Pens, paper, CD player to play the public service announcement & hip hop songs.

ICE BREAKER:
No ice breaker used in this workshop, choose one from "ice breaker" list.

WORKSHOP CORE:

PUBLIC SERVICE ANNOUNCEMENT: Read to the students (or play audio) a few real Public Service Announcements, all with themes that relate to the prison crisis, youth violence, etc. Alternate each with a stanza of a hip hop song that reflects the same message. Make the connection between creative work and possible service it could do for the community. (10 min)

RESPONSE QUESTIONS: students will respond to each question on paper. (3 min each)

1. What would you want to tell your Mother about your experiences here?

2. What would you tell your younger sibling, cousin, niece/nephew (someone that looks up to you)?

3. What would you want to tell your local politician?

4. What would you want to tell your role model?

5. What would you want to tell your old teacher, or a teacher in your life?

6. What would you want to tell your best friend?

7. What would you want to tell your worst enemy?

8. Choose one more person whom you haven't been able to speak to honestly about your recent experiences, and write down what you would want to tell them? (24 min)

GROUP ACTIVITY:
Break into groups of 3-4 to discuss and/or share their responses. Group members combine their answers, thoughts, and any questions or other sentiments this discussion brings up to create a public service announcement that can be modeled after the public service announcement we share with them. Announcement may be in the form of spoken word, lyricism, and/or poetry and should last at least 1 min. Each member should have a speaking role in radio announcement. Groups can mimic announcement format heard in class or design original format. (15 min)

WRAP UP: Each group shares the radio announcement they created. Discussion: Can radio/poetry/music change the way people think? What truths do you know that you think others should know? What issues do you want the public to hear you out on?

How is Your Change Gonna Come?

OBJECTIVES:
Begin the dialogue on how to inspire through words, encourage literacy through art, educate on Sam Cooke', create a song with two elements of inspiration; personal struggle and hope for society, understand the ability to free the inner self through lyrics.

MATERIALS:
Pen, Paper, Note Sheet on Sam Cooke's "A Change is Gonna Come", Chalk board, Prize for Icebreaker (T-Shirts or CD), CD Player, CD: Sam Cooke's "A Change is Gonna Come" and the Fugees' version of the "A Change is Gonna Come," as well as any other selection the facilitator would like to reference relating to struggle.

ICE BREAKER:
The No Game- Pin a small post-it on each person's clothes, one per person. "The object of the game is to collect the most post-its. To collect post-its, you must have an opponent say the word 'No' to you. Upon uttering that word, you may promptly collect every post-it currently pinned on them; they are yours, at least until you say 'No'. Person with the most post-its wins the game, receives a prize." (10 min)
Name that Tune Game- Break into groups of 3 or 4. Facilitator gives one word such as "brother". Teams take alternate turns singing a line from songs that contain that word. Last team to sing a song with that word wins. (10 min)

WORKSHOP CORE:
WRITE: "STRUGGLE/HOPE" in a large size on the board.

BIO: Give brief bio of Sam Cooke. (5 min)

DISCUSSION: what's the correlation between struggle and hope? Listen to "A Change is Gonna Come'. Go through notes about the song. Ask students to rhyme the lyrics (one of the verses). Highlight points concerning a struggle or the Civil Rights Movement in all verses. Highlight use of Bob Dylan as a mentor. Cooke was able to breakthrough racial dividers for creation of art & inspiration. Listen to the Fugees' version: What are the similarities and differences? (10 min)

QUESTIONS: How do you write a song that inspires? Cooke gave his own personal struggles. What were some of the artists' struggles in the songs you mentioned within the 'Name that Tune' Game? (5 min)

FREE WRITE: 1st Prompt: write a poem/verse explaining one of your struggles.(10 min)
(Observe Chorus) Cooke used his personal struggles to develop his hope for future society. What were some of the artists' struggles in the songs you mentioned at the beginning of class? Can you name a song that expresses hope? (Tupac "The Way It Is")
2nd Prompt: write a poem/line that expresses a hope for society. (10 min)

WRAP UP: Talk about the elements of self-freedom that develop during written expression. How did it feel to use your own struggle to create something that goes beyond your personal experience and has the ability to inspire many? Share pieces from class. Open Mic for poetry or songs students are inspired to perform based on work done in class. (20 min)

Resources

Organizations & Websites

Blackout Arts Collective
www.blackoutartscollective.org

New York University
Gallatin school of Individualized Study
www.nyu.edu/gallatin

Columbia University
Africana Criminal Justice Project
www.columbia.edu/cu/ccbh/acjp/

Eugene Lang College The New School for Liberal Arts
www.newschool.edu/lang

Critical Resistance
www.criticalresistance.org

Osborne Association
www.osborneny.org

Prison Moratorium Project
www.nomoreprisons.org

Friends of Island Academy
www.foiany.org

Voices Unbroken
www.voicesunbroken.org

New York State Arts in Correctional Education Network
www.nyslc.org

The Malcolm X & Dr. Betty Shabazz Memorial and Educational Center
www.theshabazzcenter.org

The Ella Baker Center
www.ellabakercenter.org

Vera Institute for Justice
www.vera.org

Sentencing & Corrections
http://www.vera.org/section3/section3_1.asp

Youth Justice
http://www.vera.org/section5/section5_1.asp

www.prisonsucks.com

www.prisonpolicy.org

www.sentencingproject.org

www.justicepolicy.org

www.360degrees.org

www.thousandkites.org

Acknowledgments

Blackout Arts Collective – Thank you for your collective vision and 10 years of arts, activism and education. Special thanks to all the artists, poets and activists who have been a part of LOL in and out of the classroom. Thank you Crystal for the dope cover! Thank you Pro for freeing the words off the page with your expert design skills. An extra special thanks to Laurent Alfred and Bryonn Bain for your leadership, guidance, honesty and passion for this work.

Island Academy, Principal Frank Dody, Assistant Principal John Curtis, Mr. Grimaldi, Ms. Roccasalvo, Ms. Mays, Mr. Reals, and the Island Academy staff. For your commitment to your students in the face of adversity and challenging the idea that students can't learn in jail. For all your support, we are deeply appreciative.

Gallatin, The Community Learning Initiative, Rene Poitevan and David Moore who first believed in the power and potential of this course. Stephen Duncombe, Mary Witty, and the Gallatin community for supporting and championing all our efforts. A special thanks to Adam Hocke, without which this definitely would not have been possible! You're amazing. Thank you to the NYU Office of Community Service for funding this project. Your support over the years has been much appreciated.

The Institute of Research in African American Studies at Columbia for supporting the very first Lyrics on Lockdown course. Special thanks to Tongo for continuing the legacy and all those who were involved in this effort.

NYU, Columbia and Lang students! Without you, this project would be incomplete. Thank you for stretching, engaging, staying true and being about the real work of artistic social justice.

A final BIG UP to all the students from Island Academy who have come week after week to get free! Thank you for keepin' it real and keeping us real. Thank you for your words, your smiles and laughter, your insight and debate. Thank you for letting us know there can be change. We look forward to the next four years.

I wish you the best and the enough.

—J.

Blackout Arts Collective (BAC) is a grassroots coalition of artists, activists and educators working to empower communities of color through the arts. We use the tools of culture and education to raise awareness and catalyze action around the critical issues that impact our communities. We believe in the power of the creative process to transform lives, mobilize communities, and build a more just society.

BAC is a national organization that operates through local action. In collaboration with other groups and campaigns that stand for justice, we continue to develop a network of artists and activists of color to foster positive social change.

Since its inception in 1997 BAC has been sustained by the love and dedication of artists, educators, and community organizers who volunteer their time, personal resources, and creativity to fulfill the mission and vision of BAC.

André Maurice Press (AMP) was founded in 2006 to provide an outlet for the published voices of the hip-hop generation. AMP is dedicated to cultivating talent, and providing writers with a means to transform their expression into a vehicle for economic empowerment.

AMP is a subsidiaray of the Owo Foro Adobe publishing and performance collaborative. Owo Foro Adobe offers book design services, manuscript coaching, and performance coaching. For more information, visit ProJones.com

We bring deferred dreams into fruition.

www.ingramcontent.com/pod-product-compliance
Lightning Source LLC
Chambersburg PA
CBHW052023290426
44112CB00014B/2354